South Dakota

AMERICA THE BEAUTIFUL

second series

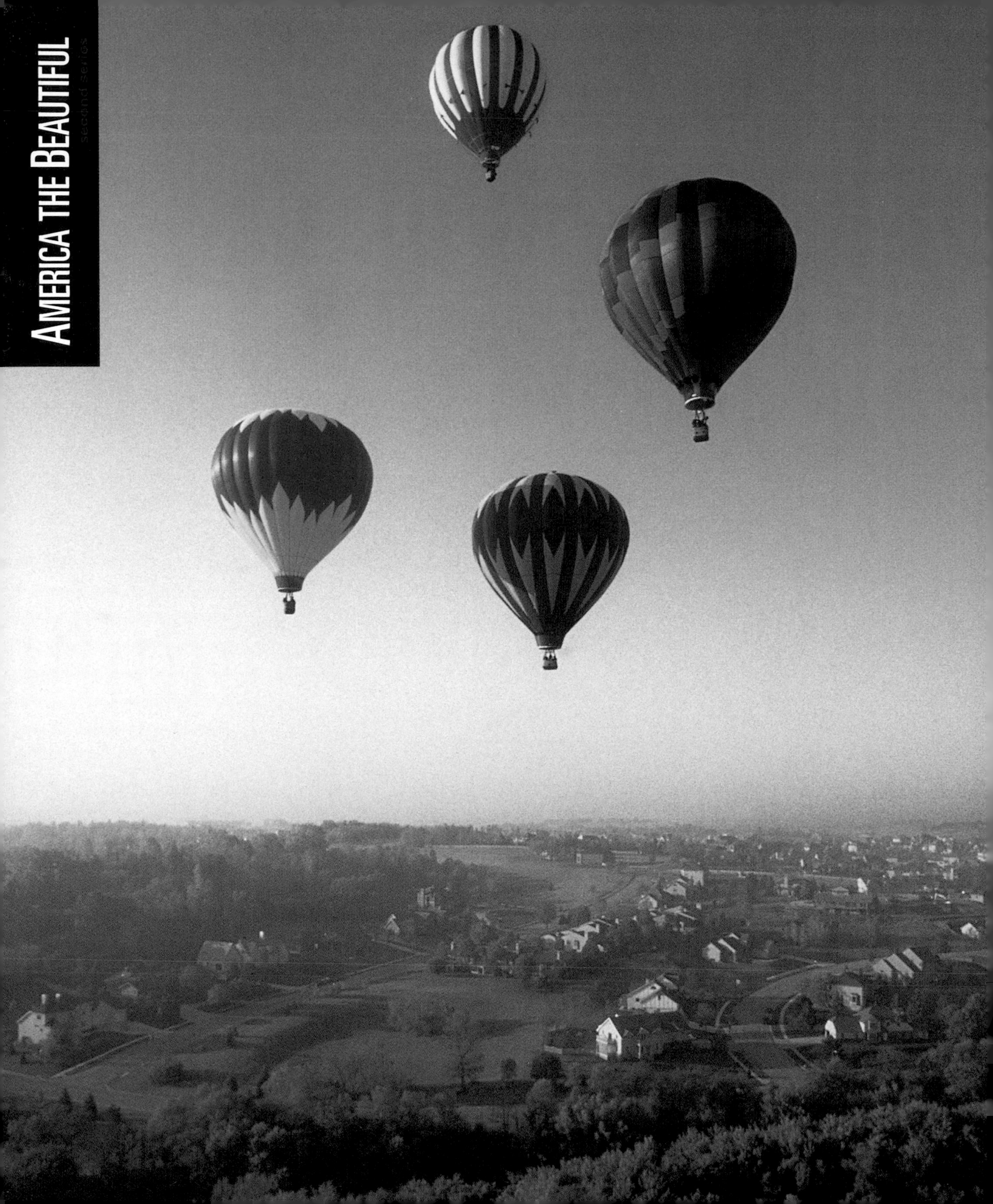

South Dakota

Donna Walsh Shepherd

Children's Press®
A Division of Grolier Publishing
New York   London   Hong Kong   Sydney
Danbury, Connecticut

Frontispiece: Balloons in Sioux Falls

Front cover: Badlands National Park

Back cover: Corn Palace in Mitchell

Consultant: Dorothy Liegl, Deputy State Librarian, South Dakota State Library

Please note: All statistics are as up-to-date as possible at the time of publication.

Visit Children's Press on the Internet at http://publishing.grolier.com

Book production by Editorial Directions, Inc.

Library of Congress Cataloging-in-Publication Data

Walsh Shepherd, Donna.
    South Dakota / Donna Walsh Shepherd.
        144 p. 24 cm.—(America the beautiful. Second series)
    Includes bibliographical references (p.) and index.
    Summary: Describes the geography, plants, animals, history, economy, religions, culture, sports, arts, and people of South Dakota.
    ISBN 0-516-21093-9
    1. South Dakota—Juvenile literature. [1. South Dakota.] I. Title. II. Series.
F651.3.W35 2001
917.83—dc21   99-054381
                                                                                      CIP
                                                                                       AC

Acknowledgments

As I was leaving the airport on my first research trip to South Dakota, I pulled off the road to check the map. The first car to pass immediately stopped, and the driver came over to see if I needed help. I said no, I was just trying to decide which was the best way to go to see the most. He then told me what was on each route, how long each would take, and his favorite things to see in the area. I quickly found that such eager helpfulness is very common in South Dakota.

I am greatly indebted to the many kind South Dakotans who patiently answered questions and who shared advice, information, and stories with me—especially Mary Stadick Smith of the Department of Tourism and Mike Mueller of the Governor's Office. They both gave me much time, help, and printed resource material. The book would not be the same without them and many others like them. Finally, I would like to thank Morris Shepherd, my husband and traveling companion, for making research trips more fun.

The Black Hills of South Dakota

Mount Rushmore

Badlands National Park

Sitting Bull

Contents

CHAPTER ONE   A Blessed Land 8

CHAPTER TWO   The Olden Days...14

CHAPTER THREE   From Sioux Wars to Statehood.......................28

CHAPTER FOUR   The Century Turns...40

CHAPTER FIVE   Land of Infinite Variety 50

CHAPTER SIX   Traveling South Dakota..................................64

CHAPTER SEVEN   The Shape of Government 80

Lake Herman

A South Dakota farm

A South Dakota mom and her sons

Lieutenant Colonel Custer

CHAPTER EIGHT   Cattle, Corn, and Computers 92

CHAPTER NINE   An Alliance of Friends 106

CHAPTER TEN   Having Fun, South Dakota Style 116

                    Timeline 128

                    Fast Facts 130

                    To Find Out More 136

                    Index 138

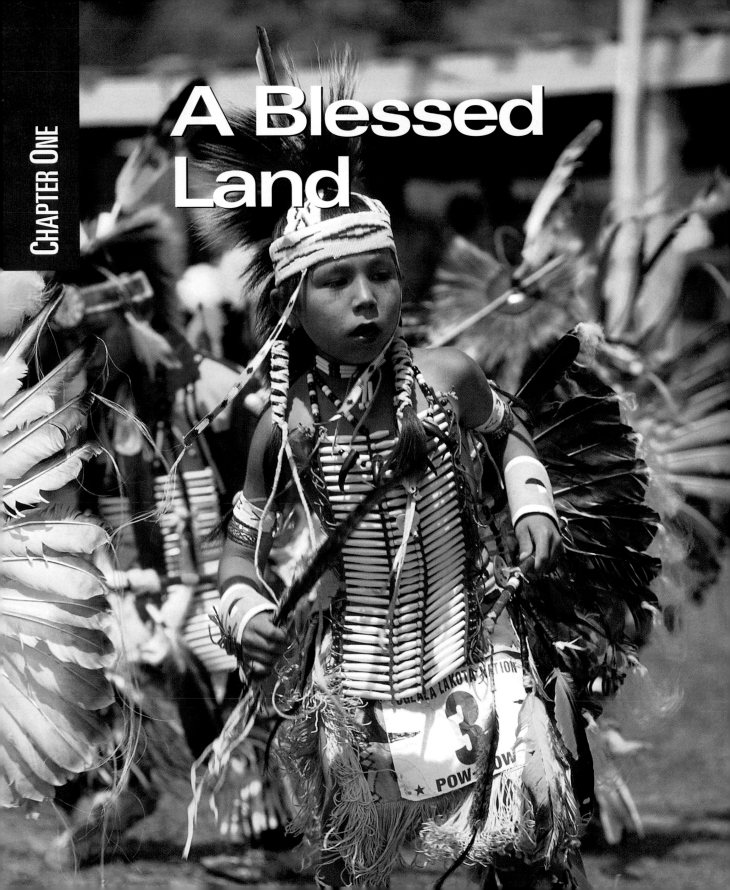

CHAPTER ONE

A Blessed Land

The young Sioux boy pulls on a pair of moccasins trimmed with beads and bells—his dancing moccasins. He grabs a tambourine in one hand and wild turkey feathers in the other and runs to join his father and grandfather. He and his family have come to this powwow, this *wacipi*, to dance in the tradition of their people, to honor their ancestors and the Great Spirit.

South Dakota's scenery can be breathtaking.

Amid drumbeats and chants, the boy and others of his tribe circle slowly, one following the other. The boy stamps his belled feet to the beat of the bison drums. Turn, shake, stomp. Turn, shake, stomp. Then he raises the feathers in his hand to the sky, as the soaring eagle rises. They dance faster now. Turn-shake-stomp. Turn-shake-stomp.

Tourists gather closer around the dancers. They come from all parts of the world to learn about Native American life on the Great Plains of South Dakota. They watch the boy and his family dance to thank the Great Spirit for many blessings: for the sun and the rain; for fresh air and freedom; and for the blessing of being Sioux and knowing the dances, which are part of a centuries-old tradition.

Opposite: A powwow at the Pine Ridge reservation

The tribe dances to ask the Great Spirit to bless their land and the lives of all present. As the sounds of chants, drumbeats, bells, and stomping all rise together, the boy hears the applause of the audience. The boy smiles, thinking that the Great Spirit also hears their sounds and will once again bless South Dakota.

Defining South Dakota

South Dakota is truly blessed with lakes and rich prairies in the east, grassland plains and the mighty Missouri in the center, and the Badlands and forested Black Hills in the west. This rich land has been home to many hardworking people. Native Americans who know the spirit of the land, farmers who grow food for America, and creative thinkers who have brought the state and nation great changes all call South Dakota home.

People in other parts of the country may know little about the state of South Dakota, but South Dakota is a part of everyone's idea of America. When people think of the old days of the Wild West, they are thinking of South Dakota. When they think of buffalo herds, the explorers Lewis and Clark, cowboys, wagon trains, and locomotives pushing westward, they are thinking of South Dakota. When they sing "Home on the Range," they are singing about South Dakota:

Oh, give me a home/where the buffalo roam
where the deer and the antelope play
where seldom is heard
a discouraging word
and the skies are not cloudy all day.

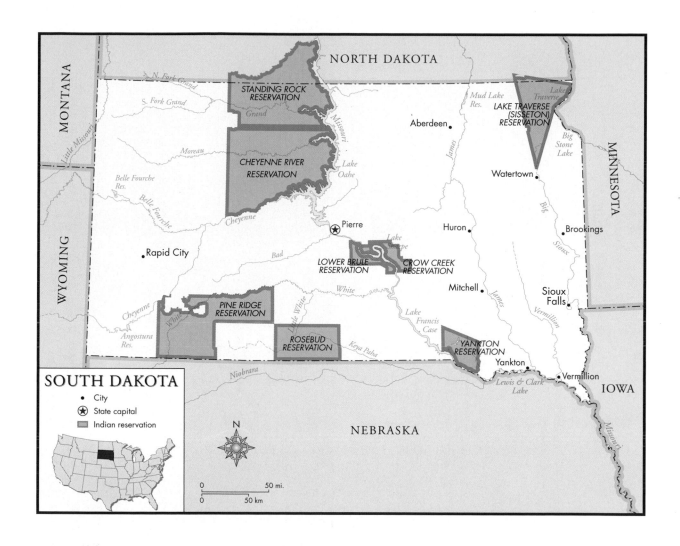

Almost everyone has seen photographs of Mount Rushmore National Memorial in southwestern South Dakota, one of the great symbols of American freedom and rights. Many people also know that a monument to Crazy Horse, the chief of the Oglala Sioux, is being carved out of a mountain in the Black Hills, not far from Mount Rushmore. When the statue is finished, it will be almost 600 feet (183 meters) high, a great symbol of pride and Native American tradition in America.

Some people have learned a little about South Dakota's history through one of America's best-loved books and television series, *Little House on the Prairie*. Many people have also heard about South Dakota's Black Hills, the Badlands, winding mysterious caves, the Pine Ridge and Rosebud Indian Reservations, the Corn Palace, and the many museums that display everything from dolls and old cars to dinosaur bones.

But people might not know that South Dakota presents world-class concerts in its new Washington Pavilion of Arts and Science in Sioux Falls and hosts the world's largest motorcycle rally in the town of Sturgis. South Dakotans sell soybeans to Japan and order buffalo burgers in local restaurants. Although South Dakota is a farming state, one of the world's largest computer manufacturers has offices there.

The people of South Dakota enjoy four seasons of fresh air and sunshine. They ride snowmobiles in winter and swim in summer. Throughout the state, they have great hunting and fishing, as well as nature preserves. The sky overhead, stretching to the far horizon, gives them a sense of space and freedom. The uncrowded cities and towns create an easy lifestyle. The crime rate is low, and trust and friendliness among neighbors are part of daily life.

South Dakota was named for the Dakota people of the great Sioux Nation. The word *dacotah* means "an alliance among friends." That is truly what the people of South Dakota are—an alliance of friends who believe that their greatest blessing is their state, one of the best places in the world to call home.

Opposite: Mount Rushmore is a well-known sight in South Dakota.

CHAPTER TWO

The Olden Days

Long before the herds of bison thundered across its plains, dinosaurs lived in what is now South Dakota. *Tyrannosaurus rex* and *Triceratops* roamed the land and fell into sinkholes, leaving behind their bones. They disappeared, along with the rest of the world's dinosaurs, about 65 million years ago. The land stood empty until many thousands of years ago, when South Dakota became home to mammoths, small horses, camels, saber-toothed tigers, and giant pigs.

Giant pigs were among the animals that roamed what is now South Dakota.

People of the Plains

Clues about South Dakota's first people date back more than 10,000 years. Scientists believe that people from Asia followed the migration routes of the mammoths and other animals across a land bridge over the Bering Strait into North America. Over time, they traveled south into the plains of South Dakota. According to some scientists, these early people, and most of the animals, may have disappeared during a period of drought—but the hunting sites and burial mounds they left behind help tell their story.

In the early sixteenth century, Plains Indian tribes began to move into the area now known as South Dakota. First, the Arikara came from the south. They lived a mostly agricultural life along the Missouri and Cheyenne Rivers. Later, the Cheyenne moved nearby.

Opposite: Settlers arriving in the South Dakota territory, 1890

In the early eighteenth century, the Ojibwa tribe in Minnesota, who had received guns from French fur traders, forced their Sioux neighbors to move south and west. After settling on the plains of South Dakota, the Sioux captured, or traded for, wild horses and lived as nomads, moving often to follow and hunt bison. For more than 100 years, the Sioux lived on the plains. Each winter, they recorded that year's history on a special bison skin, which was called the "winter count."

The seven tribes of the great Sioux Nation built a good life on the plains. But they had no idea that white people would come to their land and claim that they owned the plains and the bison. The Sioux would soon learn about these people.

La Salle proclaiming the French Empire in America

The First Explorers

In 1682, the French explorer René-Robert Cavelier, Sieur de La Salle, arrived at the mouth of the Mississippi River. He claimed the river, and all the land drained by it and all its tributaries, for the king of France. This area included most of central North America. The French built communities in the area that is now New Orleans, Louisiana, and along the St. Lawrence River in Canada. From these outposts they began to explore their new territory.

The first white men known to visit what is now South Dakota were two French brothers, François and Louis-Joseph La

The Great Sioux Nation

The name *Sioux* comes from *nadouessioux*, the Ojibwa word for their enemy, meaning "little snakes." In the eighteenth century, when the Europeans arrived in what is now South Dakota, there were seven distinct Sioux tribes—all members of the Seven Council Fire. Together, these tribes formed the great Sioux Nation.

The tribes spoke three different Sioux dialects, or related languages: Lakota, Nakota, and Dakota. They called their tribes by these names. Each language group had its own tribal structure and lived in its own part of the state. The Lakota, or Teton Sioux, lived in the central and western parts of the state. The Nakota, called Yankton or Yank-tonnais Sioux, lived in the east and southeast. The Dakota, or Santee Sioux, lived in the northeast and what is now southwestern Minnesota. These tribes were further divided into bands. For example, the Oglala are also Lakota or Teton Sioux. Today, the Sioux continue to honor the culture and traditions of the great Sioux Nation. ■

Verendrye. In 1743, the explorers buried a lead plate at the top of a hill near Fort Pierre on the Missouri River reclaiming the land for France. A group of children playing in the area in 1913 found

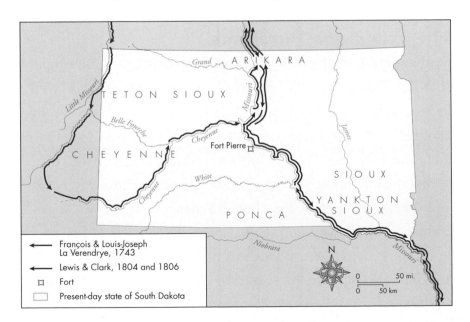

Exploration of South Dakota

Tepee—A Living Place

The Plains Indians had to move often to follow the herds of bison they hunted. To make it easier, they created the tepee, a kind of tent that could be put up or dismantled quickly. To make a tepee, they wrapped bison hides around tall poles arranged in a cone shape. These simple and practical homes also had symbolic meanings. The poles represented a man's support for his family. The covering signified a woman's shelter for her family.

Inside the tepee, smoke from the camp fire flowed up and out through open flaps in the top of the hide covering. In winter, the Indians added an inner liner and piled snow against the tepee to keep the dwelling warm. Tepees are still occasionally used as temporary homes, especially for summer camping and at festival gatherings. ■

the plate, which had been exposed by the erosion of the ground in which it was buried.

The Louisiana Purchase

Settlements in the New World proved too expensive and troublesome for France. In 1803, after Spain had owned Louisiana briefly, France sold the United States all the land that La Salle had claimed. Although there was little money in the U.S. Treasury at that time, President Thomas Jefferson couldn't pass up the chance to buy the Louisiana Territory—called the Louisiana Purchase—and double the size of the United States. Jefferson was a great enthusiast of the West and studied every book he could find about it. In 1804, he chose two U.S. Army officers, Meriwether Lewis and William Clark, to travel west to explore the newly purchased territory.

The Corps of Discovery

Lewis and Clark's expedition, known as the Corps of Discovery, entered what is now South Dakota on August 21, 1804. One of the members wrote that the region was a "Garden of Eden." Except for one tense encounter with the Sioux Indians, the explorers met peacefully with Native Americans who offered supplies and advice.

Sacagawea points the way to Lewis and Clark.

During the fifty-four days they spent in the region, members of the expedition collected and studied the area's animals and plants. They spent one full day trying to capture a live prairie dog, which they called a "barking squirrel." They sent the prairie dog and some buffalo hides back to President Jefferson. He was thrilled with their news about the West—and so pleased with the buffalo hides that he hung them in the entryway of his house in Monticello, Virginia.

Two years later, on August 21, 1806, the explorers reentered South Dakota on their trip home. This time, they were traveling downstream and spent only two weeks in the area.

The Settlers Arrive

Many adventurers and trappers followed Lewis and Clark. By 1817, Joseph La Framboise had established a permanent trading post on the west bank of the Missouri at what is now Fort Pierre.

Sacagawea

Sacagawea was only twelve years old when the Hidatsa tribe kidnapped her from her Shoshone home in Idaho and sold her as a slave. Later, Toussaint Charbonneau, a French-Canadian fur trapper, won her in a gambling bet and made her one of his wives.

When Sacagawea was fifteen years old and eight months pregnant, Lewis and Clark hired her husband as an interpreter. Although they hired him, they really wanted Sacagawea. Clark thought that traveling with a woman and a baby would show the Indians they met along the way that the expedition came in peace. He also hoped she might convince the Shoshone to sell them some horses.

Sacagawea traveled with the group—carrying her baby—and acted as guide, interpreter, food gatherer, and adviser. Her loyalty, cheerfulness, and courage quickly won everyone's respect. When one of the boats nearly capsized, she saved the expedition's records and supplies. She also showed them shortcuts through mountain passes.

In the Rockies, the travelers met a group of Shoshone Indians. The chief was Sacagawea's brother. After celebrations, Sacagawea arranged for the purchase of the horses. When the group continued on, she stayed with the expedition. When they neared the Pacific Ocean, the party voted to camp inland. But Sacagawea had dreamed of seeing the ocean. When word came that a whale had washed ashore, she insisted that she be allowed to go see both.

After returning to the Missouri River Valley, Sacagawea died at age twenty-six, at Fort Manual in South Dakota, of a long illness. William Clark adopted her two children. A memorial to her stands near Chief Sitting Bull's grave on the Standing Rock Reservation. This memorial is not her only honor, however. Two hundred years after her birth, the likenesses of Sacagawea and her son were printed on the U.S. Golden Dollar issued in 2000—a testimonial to her contributions to the Lewis and Clark Expedition and to the young United States. ■

In 1831, the *Yellowstone*, the first steamboat on the Missouri, sailed upstream to the trading post to buy furs. As river travel became easier, more visitors arrived. Among them were the naturalist and artist John James Audubon, famous for his paintings of birds; Alexander Philipp Maximilian, the prince of Weid-Neuweid (now in Germany); and artist Karl Bodmer. Maximilian, a world traveler, came to explore the territory west of the Mississippi River and to study its Indian people. He brought Bodmer with him to illustrate the book he planned to write about his travels.

After the explorers and adventurers came the farmers. Soon, conflicts arose between the settlers who wanted to take over land for farming and ranching and the Indians who had hunted on the

Painter John James Audubon spent time in the territory west of the Mississippi River.

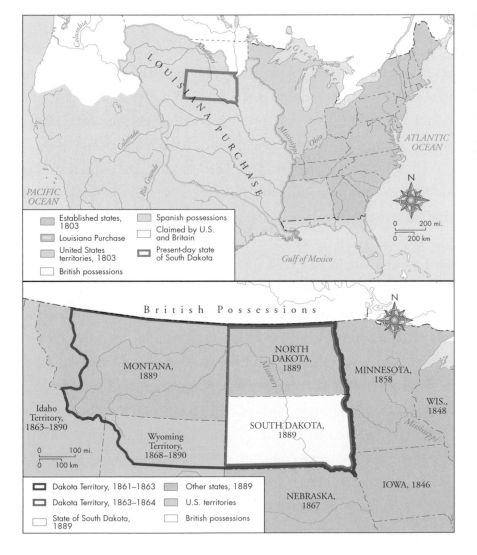

Historical maps of South Dakota

land for centuries. As more and more prairie grass disappeared under the farmer's plow, the Sioux and the bison were pushed farther and farther west.

As they fought to save their way of life, the Indians raided settlements, burning buildings, sometimes killing the newcomers. The Indian raids temporarily discouraged settlers, but soon more farmers and ranchers began to arrive. The U.S. government offered to make treaties with the Indians, buy their land, and establish areas reserved only for Native Americans. The Indians, however, believed that land could not belong to anyone and therefore could not be bought or sold. They did not understand what the white man's words and treaties would bring an end to their way of life.

Under government pressure, the Yankton and Santee Sioux sold much of their traditional land and moved to the reservations that the government had established. The United States promised that Indians living on reservations would be safe from land-hungry settlers and would be given food and supplies, which were now scarce because the bison were almost gone. At first, the move to the reservations solved some of the conflicts between settlers and Native Americans. But some settlers didn't know—or didn't care— that an area was reserved as Indian land, and many tribes did not feel obliged to keep promises made by another tribe's chief.

In 1861, Congress established the Dakota Territory, which included what are now South Dakota, North Dakota, and much of Wyoming and Montana. Yankton, where the James River meets the Missouri at the southeast corner of the territory, became the territorial capital. To encourage expansion and further settlement in all the western territories, Congress passed the Homestead Act in

1862. After building a house and working the land for five years, a farmer could claim 160 acres (65 hectares) of land. People flocked into the Dakota Territory, especially Irish, German, and Scandinavian immigrants. They settled on the prairie, offering hard work as the down payment for a better life.

Yankton in 1865

The Bison Vanish

As more and more people traveled west, blankets made of bison skin, called buffalo robes, became popular in the East. White hunters shot bison for the hides and for sport. Some soldiers and hunters competed to see who could shoot the most bison in a day.

Hunting the bison

Sodbusters

Plowing prairie land for the first time was very difficult. The deep prairie-grass roots were so tightly matted that farmers often had to chop the ground ahead of the plow with an ax. Those matted roots turned out to be a great help, however—they were used to build homes on the vast treeless prairie.

The settlers were able to cut bricks of dirt from the root-bound top layer of the grassy soil. They built the walls of their homes with these sod bricks, adding a store-bought door and window. They piled more sod on the wood-plank roofs. The houses were cool in the summer and, with a stove inside, warm in the winter. However, they tended to be dirty and could actually dissolve in heavy rains! These early settlers became known as sodbusters, and their houses were called "soddies." ■

They took the animals' skins and tongues, a gourmet delicacy, and left the carcasses to rot on the prairie. The U.S. Army encouraged this wasteful killing. They thought the Indians would be forced to move to reservations when no bison were left to support the Indian way of life.

The Sioux people, who considered the bison to be their spiritual brothers, saw this killing as a great wrong. The Indians believed that bison should be respected and protected. They did not kill bison unless they needed the meat to live.

Before the Europeans arrived, millions of bison roamed the plains from Canada to Texas. By 1890, the slaughter was so complete that only 541 bison remained.

Chief Red Cloud's War

As the Sioux watched their land and their way of life vanish, they became angry and desperate. They increased the number of raids against trespassing settlers and travelers. Chief Red Cloud, a great Indian warrior, led the fight to stop travel and settlement in the Black Hills—especially along the Bozeman Trail to Montana. For years, he and his warriors attacked pioneers traveling west, making settlement in the Black Hills impossible.

In 1868, the U.S. government signed the Fort Laramie Treaty, which finally ended Red Cloud's war. The treaty met Red Cloud's terms by establishing the great Sioux Nation and giving the Teton Sioux all the land west of the Missouri River to the Bighorn Mountains at the Wyoming border. The sacred Black Hills would be Sioux land forever. According to the treaty, the U.S. government

Chief Red Cloud tried to protect the Black Hills.

promised to abandon its army post in the area, protect the Sioux from encroaching settlers, and provide the Sioux with food, clothing, health care, and education.

Gold Rush

In 1848, a tribal leader in the Southern Black Hills area had presented the missionary Father Pierre-Jean de Smet with a small leather bag. De Smet looked in the bag, and he was horrified by what he saw—gold dust! He knew what would happen if word got out that there was gold in the region. He quickly gave the bag back to the Native American chief and warned him, "Put it away and show it to nobody."

Father de Smet

Hiding that bag of Black Hills gold didn't make much difference, though. Eventually, gold was discovered in Montana, and in 1873, the Northern Pacific Railroad began surveying for a railroad that would travel through Sioux land to Montana's goldfields. The proposed route was a clear violation of the Fort Laramie Treaty. Sioux warriors attacked, which made it difficult to continue building the railway. Ignoring the treaty terms, the railroad company and the Dakota Territory legislature asked Congress to send troops to control the Indians and protect the workers. Congress sent Lieutenant Colonel George Armstrong Custer.

At first, Custer and his troops didn't have much trouble with the Indians, so they spent their time exploring the territory and looking for gold. After the great 1848 California gold strike, people began looking for gold throughout the West. The Black Hills gave them just what they wanted. In an 1874 report to his commanding officer in Bismarck, Custer wrote that gold seemed to be everywhere in the Black Hills. A Chicago newspaper found out about the report and published a story telling readers that Custer's party had found gold in the Black Hills. A new gold rush was on—right in the heart of sacred Sioux territory.

Lieutenant Colonel Custer

CHAPTER THREE

From Sioux Wars to Statehood

After the discovery of gold, fortune seekers poured into the Black Hills. Once again, the treaty the U.S. government had signed with Chief Red Cloud was ignored. And once again, the Sioux were forced to protect their land themselves. They raided the mining camps and the travelers who were trespassing on Indian land. To stop the raids, the government offered to buy the Black Hills for $6 million or pay $400,000 for the right to mine the area for gold. The Sioux refused. They would not sell their sacred land.

Sitting Bull resisted going to a reservation.

Forced Move

The U.S. government wanted peace. It decided that the easiest way to achieve it was to move all Native Americans out of the miners' way and onto reservations. The army tried to force all the Sioux people onto reservations immediately.

Some of the Indians, who no longer wanted to fight, moved to the reservations and tried to live by farming, as the government said they must. The reservation land was often the poorest land available, however, and was not well suited to farming. Because the Sioux were used to an independent and nomadic lifestyle, many hated the idea of being confined to a reservation. For them, it was like being in jail.

Opposite: The Battle of the Little Bighorn

Song of the Earth

The U.S. government believed that Native Americans could quickly change from being hunters on the plains to farmers on reservations. The traditions, values, and beliefs of the Sioux—which were deeply rooted in their way of life—were not so easily changed, however. The Indians' strong and sacred relationship to the land is revealed in this beautiful poem, thought to be written by Chief Joseph of the Nez Percé tribe:

You ask me to plow the ground.
Shall I take a knife and tear my
*   mother's breast?*
Then when I die
She will not take me to her
*   bosom to sleep.*

You ask me to dig for stone.
Shall I dig under her skin for
*   bones?*
Then when I die
I cannot enter her body to be
*   born again.*

You ask me to cut grass and make
*   hay,*
And sell it and be rich like the
*   white man.*
But how dare I cut off my
*   mother's hair.*
It is a bad law and my people can-
*   not obey it!*

Two Sioux leaders—Sitting Bull and Crazy Horse—refused to move to the reservations. The army continually attacked the tribes of these chiefs, trying to force them to move onto reservations.

Life on the plains became harder and harder for the Sioux. With the bison nearly gone, they had lost their main food supply. They had not, however, lost their strong spirit. In 1876, many tribes gathered for a celebration and Sun Dance at the Little Bighorn River in what is now Montana. The army found out about the gathering and saw it as an opportunity to force more Indians onto reservations.

Although General Alfred H. Terry ordered Custer to wait before taking action, Custer decided on a surprise attack. He greatly underestimated the size of the Indian encampment. As he attacked, the warriors quickly responded, led by Chiefs Gall and Crazy Horse and with spiritual guidance from Chief Sitting Bull. In a fierce battle, Custer and all his men were killed. The Battle of the Little Bighorn became known as "Custer's Last Stand" and was the last major battle won by the Sioux.

Chief Gall fought in what is known as Custer's Last Stand.

On the Reservations

After the Sioux victory in the Battle of the Little Bighorn, the army hunted the Indians relentlessly. The starving tribes were no match for the large, well-armed U.S. Army. Finally, in May 1877, Crazy Horse and more than 1,000 of his followers voluntarily moved to a reservation. In the proud tradition of Crazy Horse, they went singing war songs and waving their weapons.

A few months later, soldiers arrested Crazy Horse as a troublemaker. When they tried to jail him at Fort Robinson, Nebraska, he resisted and was fatally stabbed in the stomach by a soldier's bayonet.

Life was as difficult on the reservation as it was off. The government continually cut its budget for the care of Native Americans, and dishonest government agents kept large sums of the money and bought substandard supplies for the reservations. And as more white settlers came, the government forced the tribes to sell even more of their land. The Indians' future seemed hopeless.

Performing the Ghost Dance

The Ghost Dance

In 1889, in the midst of all this despair, Wovoka, a Paiute Indian prophet, had a dream. He dreamed that the white people were going away and the buffalo were returning. He dreamed that all the Indians who had been killed by soldiers had come back to life. Prophetic dreams and visions were important to the Sioux and were taken very seriously.

As news of Wovoka's dream spread, Indians across the plains danced the Ghost Dance, a form of prayer, to help the prophet's vision come true. The Ghost Dance made the U.S. Army very nervous. They thought the sacred dance was a war dance. They thought the swaying Indians dressed in white were preparing to begin more raids. To stop the dancing, the army decided to arrest Sitting Bull, a respected spiritual leader of the Sioux Nation. When the reservation police arrested him on December 15, 1890, Sitting Bull broke free and shooting began. Chief Sitting Bull and thirteen others—including Sitting Bull's seventeen-year-old son Crow Foot—were killed.

Wounded Knee

After their leader had been killed, hundreds of Sitting Bull's followers fled the reservation. The army set out to round them up and permanently stop the Ghost Dance. Many Indians decided to take refuge with Chief Big Foot on the Cheyenne River Reservation—but the soldiers got there first. On December 28, 1890, Chief Big Foot and his 350 followers tried to slip out of camp and away from the soldiers. The soldiers caught up with them the next day near Wounded Knee Creek.

The soldiers surrounded the band and began to take their few weapons away. As one Indian began a Ghost Dance, someone fired a shot. Immediately, soldiers were shooting at any and all Indians—the elders running, small children standing crying, pregnant women, people already shot. Even soldiers who got in the way were shot by other soldiers.

Native Americans suffered defeat at the Battle of Wounded Knee.

In the end, nearly 300 Indians and 30 U.S. soldiers were killed. The soldiers received medals and honorable funerals. A few days later, the Indians were buried in a mass grave at Wounded Knee. Buried with them were the hopes and spirit of the traditional Indian way of life.

Striking It Rich

While the army fought the Indians, the miners were busy finding gold and spending money. Within months of the Chicago newspaper's announcement, 25,000 people arrived in the Black Hills. Mining towns sprang up everywhere. They included towns such as

The city of Deadwood in 1876

Custer, where gold was first found; Lead (pronounced Leed), named after a geological formation that often leads to gold veins; and Deadwood, one of the wildest towns in the West.

Many miners were successful, but the most successful were Moses and Fred Manuel and their partner, Hank Harney. These men staked a 5-acre (2-ha) claim at Lead and discovered one of the richest veins of gold in North America. That claim became the centerpiece of the Homestake Mine, one of the richest gold mines in the world.

Wild Bill and Calamity Jane

poker and make money. And he did—until the day he broke his own rule and sat at a poker table with his back to the door. Jack McCall—who wanted to be famous, too—walked in the door and shot Hickok in the back. Seven months later, McCall was hanged at Yankton for the crime.

Another Deadwood legend was Martha Canary, better known as Calamity Jane (right). She was well known for her excellent riding, shooting, drinking, and swearing. She once said that to offend her was to ask for "calamity"—which is how she got her name. For some time, she toured the world with the Buffalo Bill Wild West Show.

Although Calamity Jane was in the Black Hills of South Dakota at the same time as Hickok, it is unlikely they knew each other well—if at all. Because both of them became legends, however, gossip linked them together to make an even better story. Today, people often think of them as a romantic couple. They are buried next to each other in Deadwood's Mount Moriah Cemetery. ■

After the gold rush, lawlessness quickly became the rule in the once-sacred Black Hills. Among the many wild characters attracted to the region was James Butler "Wild Bill" Hickok (above). Wild Bill was an Indian scout, soldier, and marshal best known as one of the fastest shots in the West. He traveled to Deadwood to play

A Plague of Locusts

During the drought years of the 1870s, massive clouds of grasshoppers, called migratory locusts, swept across the land, eating every green thing in their path. Behind them, they left fields of stubble and financial ruin. To save their crops, farmers tried to burn areas around their fields to keep the grasshoppers from coming that way. They also dug long trenches across the land and poured oil into them. The locusts that fell in the trenches would get stuck there. Then, the farmers set fire to the trenches, burning the locusts and the eggs that would have hatched the next year. Because of pesticides, today's farmers no longer have to worry about swarms of locusts destroying their crops. This type of grasshopper no longer exists in the United States. ■

The Farming Life

As the army pushed the Indians onto reservations and the miners partied in the saloons of Deadwood, life on the eastern South Dakota farms and the western South Dakota ranches remained difficult. Some years brought droughts, and the crops withered. Some years brought floods, and the crops drowned or rotted. Other years, there were Indian raids or insects to worry about.

Settlers flocked to the Dakota Territory to make a new life, but in the face of such hardships, many gave up and left. Only the toughest and most determined succeeded in the Dakota Territory.

Sheep and cattle ranchers came to the western part of the territory to raise livestock on the grasslands that once nourished bison. Ranchers branded their animals to show their ownership and then let them run free, feeding across the range until it was time to go to market. The cattlemen resented the sheep ranchers, however. They thought the sheep were killing the grass, because they ate the grass down to the roots. Cattle only chewed off the blades. For a time, this dispute led to range wars between sheep ranchers and cattle ranchers. Soon, to settle arguments, barbed-wire fences began dividing up the Wild West.

Branding is a way to mark the ownership of cattle.

Statehood

In the 1850s, the people of the Dakota Territory were eager to qualify for statehood. They wanted the military and financial support that the states enjoyed. They even exaggerated their population numbers in order to qualify, but that scheme didn't work.

As part of the 1868 Fort Laramie Treaty, the borders for the Wyoming and Montana Territories were carved out of the Dakota Territory. The Dakota Territory then began seriously working on becoming a state. It took another twenty-one years of building a stable farming community and increasing its population before Congress finally took the Dakota Territory seriously.

Two groups worked for statehood, under different terms. One group wanted to make the Dakota Territory a single state; the

The Fortieth State?

South Dakota was the fortieth state admitted to the Union. Or was it the thirty-ninth? North and South Dakota entered the Union together—but before signing the two statehood bills, newly elected President Benjamin Harrison shuffled the papers. Harrison said, "They were born together. They are one and I will make them twins." No one—not even Harrison—knew which state bill he signed first. To solve the dilemma, the two states were admitted in alphabetical order. North Dakota became the thirty-ninth state, and South Dakota became the fortieth. ■

other group wanted to divide the territory into two states. In 1883, the group calling itself the South Dakotans wrote a separate constitution and pushed for statehood, but it was denied. In 1885, they pushed harder with a new constitution. Again, statehood was denied.

In the elections of 1888, the Republican Party won control of the U.S. Congress. The Dakota Territory was heavily Republican, so Congress supported admitting the territory as two states. It hoped that as two states, the territory would send four Republican senators to Congress, not just two.

Finally, on February 20, 1889, the Omnibus Bill was passed, allowing Washington, Montana, North Dakota, and South Dakota to become states. President Grover Cleveland signed the bill with a quill pen made from a Dakota Territory eagle feather. On November 2, 1889, North Dakota and South Dakota officially became states. Arthur Mellette, the territorial governor, became the first state governor, and Pierre became the capital—but not without argument.

Choosing a Capital

Nearly every town in the new state of South Dakota wanted the honor—and the economic advantages—of being the new capital. Each one mounted campaigns and formed alliances to convince the rest of the state that it was the best choice.

The town of Pierre had very little going for it—not much commerce and a small population—but it had one major advantage. Pierre was located in the center of the state. Because of its position, in 1889 voters finally decided to make Pierre the temporary capital. Over the next few years, no other city could get the necessary support, so, in 1904, Pierre became the permanent capital of South Dakota.

The city of Pierre in 1892

CHAPTER FOUR

The Century Turns

South Dakota had a troublesome beginning as a state. In its early years, it suffered the tragedy of Wounded Knee, faced several discouraging droughts, and endured weak farm prices. As the new century began, however, rains and optimism returned. During World War I (1914–1918), troops needed South Dakota's meat, grains, and produce. Farming profits soared. People increased their production and cheered their way into the prosperous period known as the Roaring Twenties.

Gutzon Borglum working on his first model of Mount Rushmore

The Rushmore Story

People working in other industries throughout the state wanted the same good fortune that the farmers and ranchers enjoyed. By that time, tourism was growing in America. State historian Doane Robinson felt that a spectacular attraction would bring visitors to South Dakota—and he knew just the thing.

He looked at the granite pillars in the Black Hills, called the Needles, and visualized the faces of famous Western explorers and Indian chiefs carved into them. His vision led him to the sculptor Gutzon Borglum. The idea intrigued Borglum, but he felt that such grand sculptures should have national subjects rather than local ones.

Borglum began scouting the Black Hills area. The Needles

Opposite: Lincoln's face being carved at Mount Rushmore

were too unstable to carve, but he found good, solid granite at Mount Rushmore. He accepted a $250 check from the Rapid City Commercial Club to begin work.

Robinson, Borglum, and Senator Peter Norbeck of South Dakota decided to tell the story of the nation with a sculpture of four presidents. George Washington would represent the birth of the nation. Thomas Jefferson, purchaser of the Louisiana Territory, would represent its growth. Abraham Lincoln, who held the country together during the Civil War (1861–1865), would represent the preservation of the United States. Theodore Roosevelt, the force behind building the Panama Canal, would represent the U.S. role in the modern world. Together, these four presidents would become the Shrine of Democracy.

Doane Robinson

Carving Mount Rushmore

On August 10, 1927, President Coolidge dedicated the project, saying, "We have come here to dedicate a cornerstone that was laid by the hand of the Almighty." Over the next fourteen years, fundraising, drilling, and blasting changed the shape of that mountain. One carver commented, "More and more we sensed that we were creating a truly great thing."

Sculptor Borglum died in March 1941, but his son Lincoln supervised the completion of the faces until October of that year. When the United States entered World War II (1939–1945), the carving stopped due to lack of money and workers. The sculpture, which was designed to show the four presidents from head to waist, remains unfinished today.

In 1997, the Mount Rushmore National Memorial park area was remodeled. Among the additions were a new entrance; a grand amphitheater where visitors can watch the lighting ceremony on summer nights; an exhibition hall; a museum; theaters; a 0.5-mile (0.8-kilometer) trail to the base of the sculpture; and—as testimony to the popularity of the site—a multilevel parking garage.

Lincoln Borglum finished the faces of the Mount Rushmore project after his father's death.

The Great Depression

The 1930s hit America hard. The country's optimism and farm prices crashed with the stock market in 1929. In South Dakota, great dust storms blew across the prairies. The sun blazed day after day, and the rains didn't come. Crops withered and died, leaving little feed for the cattle. With nothing to sell, farmers' debts accumulated. The next year, it was the same; only the debts grew. Then the clouds of locusts returned. For some people, it was too much—too much prairie, too much sky, too many troubles. As people began losing their farms and homes, they packed up and left South Dakota, only to find that times were hard all over the United States.

A farm after a dust storm

To ease the country's suffering, President Franklin D. Roosevelt started a group of state-relief programs known as the New Deal. Thirty-nine percent of all South Dakotans—a greater percentage than in any other state—got help surviving the crashing economy. Federal public-work programs funded jobs that helped South Dakota build roads, schools, and bridges and improve its national parks. In 1934, the government passed the Indian Reorganization Act, returning some land to the tribes and giving Native Americans on reservations the right to govern themselves. The government also raised the official price of gold from $20 to $35 an ounce (31 grams), which started another mining boom in the Black Hills.

Wartime and the Years After

The hard times of the Great Depression continued until World War II broke out. Once again, troops needed South Dakota's meat, grains, and produce. Farmers worked overtime. Two new military bases opened in the state—Ellsworth Air Force Base near Rapid City and Sioux Falls Air Force Training Base. Once again, war had saved the state's economy.

After the war, the government set out to solve some of its recurring problems: drought, flooding along the Missouri and Mississippi Rivers, and the need for more electrical power. In a major

Into the Space Age

The excitement generated by airplanes during World War II reached new heights in South Dakota in 1935. The National Geographic Society and the U.S. Army Air Corps worked together to create a balloon that could explore the stratosphere for the first time.

One of the team members knew of a deep, natural bowl away from dangerous winds outside Rapid City. There, the balloon could safely be inflated and launched. On the night of November 10, under giant floodlights, Indian chiefs gave a blessing and the helium gas tanks began pumping. It took all night to fill the balloon (right), which was made with 2.6 acres (1.1 ha) of cloth and—including gondola, equipment, and crew—weighed 15,000 pounds (6,810 kilograms).

At 7 A.M., the ropes that held the huge balloon to the ground were untied, and it floated skyward. This first space flight captivated America. Everyone listened to its progress on the radio. The balloon and its two pilots soared 72,395 feet (22,080 m) into the air—nearly 14 miles (23 km). After collecting data in the stratosphere for 2.5 hours, the crew began releasing helium and slowly descended. Eight hours after taking off, they were met by cheering crowds in an eastern South Dakota farm field, 240 miles (386 km) away from their starting point. The space age had officially begun. ■

project that lasted from 1944 to 1966, four dams were built on the Missouri River in South Dakota. Today, these dams continue to provide hydroelectric power and irrigation water and help control flooding. They have also become popular recreation areas. The reservoir lakes—Oahe, Francis Case, Sharpe, and Lewis and Clark—are known as the Great Lakes of South Dakota. Together, they have more shoreline than California has coastline.

Farming Today

Farming has changed since the sodbuster days. Computers have now entered the field. They provide farmers with better information

High technology is used on today's farms.

about methods of irrigation, seeds, and animals. Computers track prices, irrigation flow, and weather conditions. They design nutritious food that they automatically feed to the animals. Farmers find the latest research on the Internet and join chat rooms to discuss where to get the best prices or which grains are best for crop rotation. Today, computer spreadsheets are as important to most farmers as spreaders for fertilizer.

Many farmers have college degrees in agriculture and business. They watch the changing prices of foreign currency as closely as the weather. They experiment with techniques to improve all aspects of farming. To reduce wind erosion of the soil, some farmers now use no-till farming.

In no-till farming, the stubble from the previous year's harvest "overwinters"—remains on the ground through the winter. In spring, instead of tilling, or turning over the soil, computerized equipment drills holes into the ground through the stubble and plants new seeds. The stubble protects the soil from blowing away or rapidly drying out. And as the plant matter rots, it also adds nutrients to the soil.

Weather Disasters

Even today, South Dakota's weather can be a deadly force. In 1972, heavy rains and flooding caused the Canyon Lake Dam near

One Evening in Spencer

In the late evening of May 30, 1998, the clouds above Spencer turned a deep blue. Then they darkened to black. The rains started, and hail soon followed. Before long, the 320 people of Spencer saw just what they didn't want to see. Funnel clouds began descending from the base of the thunderstorm. As the clouds grew into tornadoes and started moving, people ran for cover. They knew this wouldn't be good—but they had no idea how bad it could get.

A total of six tornadoes touched down in Spencer. Two of them joined together, strengthening to a multivortex F-4 class tornado with winds of 220 miles (354 km) per hour. The tornado roared across the countryside and right through Spencer, ripping up the ground and everything in it and on it.

By 9 P.M., the tornado had run out of steam. Darkness and rain replaced the winds. Six people had died, half the population was injured, and nearly every building, business, and home was destroyed or had vanished—splintered across the prairie.

By May 1999, just one year after the disaster, Spencer was a checkerboard of vacant lots and new buildings with new lawns and small new trees. Other than the few buildings that it missed, the only thing the tornado left behind in Spencer was the townspeople's South Dakotan determination. ■

Rapid City to break, killing 238 people and washing away $100 million of property. Flooding in other areas that same year caused several deaths and an estimated $750 million damage to homes and crops.

In 1993, Governor George S. Mickelson and seven other people were killed when their small plane developed mechanical trouble during bad weather and crashed. In 1998, the town of Spencer nearly disappeared in a tornado. As scientists work for better warning and protection systems, South Dakotans never forget that Mother Nature is in charge.

Native Americans Today

Since the Indian Reorganization Act of 1934, which made all Native Americans citizens of the United States, Native American pride, languages, and customs have been reviving. Conditions on

Native Americans try to retain their traditions in the modern world.

the reservations, however, are still quite poor. Rates of unemployment, poverty, alcoholism, school dropouts, and infant deaths there are among the worst in the nation.

In 1973, a group from the American Indian Movement held a protest at Wounded Knee on the Pine Ridge Reservation. The protest lasted seventy-one days. After two deaths and hundreds of arrests, the group and the government agreed to meet to discuss the plight of Native Americans.

South Dakotans, both native and nonnative, continue to work to solve these problems. Programs for jobs, education, and health care have helped. In 1990, 100 years after the battle at Wounded Knee, Governor George S. Mickelson and tribal leaders declared a Year of Reconciliation. The next year, they declared a Century of Reconciliation.

The Alliance of Tribal Tourism, formed in 1992, helps promote Native American art and crafts, powwows, visits to reservations, and the establishment of casinos. These efforts have provided badly needed jobs and income—but they are only a start. In 1999, President Bill Clinton visited the Pine Ridge Reservation, the poorest county in the nation. After seeing the conditions there, he pledged to provide additional support.

The Next Century

As the century turned again, the concerns of South Dakotans remained much the same as they had been in 1900: family, cultural

A New Battle for the Black Hills

After moving to the reservations, Crazy Horse and Sitting Bull probably never would have guessed that the battles to regain their lands lay ahead. However, their descendants would fight these in the courtroom—not on the prairie. In 1980, the U.S. Supreme Court finally ruled that the 1868 Fort Laramie Treaty with the Indians had been broken and that the Black Hills had been taken illegally.

According to the treaty, 75 percent of all Sioux men had to approve any changes made to the treaty. When the United States took the Black Hills, only 10 percent of the Sioux had signed their approval. In its ruling, the Court wrote, "A more ripe and rank case of dishonorable dealings will never, in all probability, be found in our history." The court ruled that the U.S. government must pay more than $100 million in damages to the Sioux. The Sioux have refused payment, however. Instead, they continue to fight for the return of 1 million acres (405,000 ha) of Black Hills National Forest. ■

heritage, farm support, and the ability to make a decent living and get a good education.

Even with modern methods, farming is a difficult way to make a living. In some states, corporations have taken over struggling family farms and combined them into factory farms. Some of these large operations produce a great amount of pollution. In 1999, to control this and support family farms, South Dakotans voted to limit how much land a corporation can farm or ranch.

Farming remains an important industry in South Dakota.

Holding onto old traditions while embracing new technology is tricky. But if anyone can do it, it's the descendants of South Dakota's sodbusters, ranchers, miners, and Native Americans.

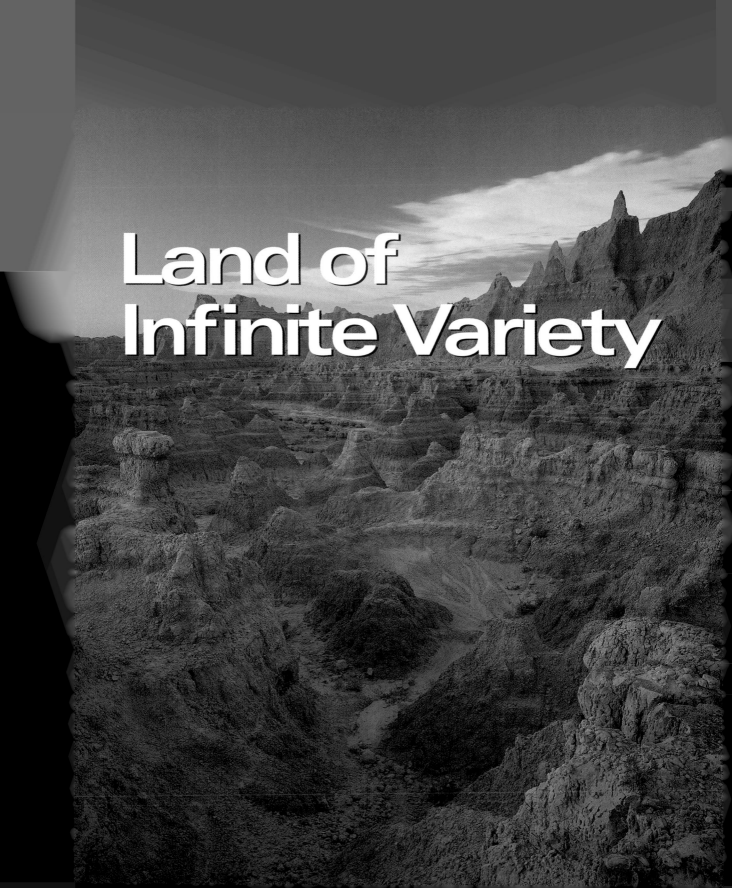

Land of
Infinite Variety

The Missouri River railroad bridge

When people say, "South Dakota? Where is that?" the correct answer is, "Smack dab in the middle of everywhere." North to south, this Midwestern state is halfway between the North Pole and the equator. East to west, it is halfway between Asia and Europe. The geographic center of the fifty states is in northwest South Dakota, 17 miles (27 km) west of Castle Rock.

One of the northern plains states, South Dakota is America's sixteenth largest state, with an area of 77,121 square miles (199,743 sq km). Ten percent of the state's territory, nearly 5 million acres (2 million ha), is reservation land.

South Dakota is bordered on the north by its companion state, North Dakota, and to the south by Nebraska. To the west are Montana and Wyoming; to the east, Minnesota and Iowa. Flowing through the middle of South Dakota—almost dividing it in half—is the great Missouri River. South Dakotans identify the two sides of their state as East River and West River. The river also seems to separate the eastern farms from the western ranches, and—as in the days of Lewis and Clark—the more settled East from the more rugged West.

Opposite: Badlands National Park

Sunflowers grace
many South Dakota
fields.

From Plains to Peaks

The central lowlands of South Dakota are in the east. This fairly flat area has rich farming soil, left by the melting glaciers that once covered the land. Water from the glaciers filled the low areas, creating marshes and hundreds of pothole and kettle lakes.

In the west, the land rises, gradually becoming drier. Grasslands line the banks of the Missouri. These plains provide both grazing land and farmland. Fields of wheat, corn, and blooming sunflowers grow from horizon to horizon. Farther west, the plains become drier yet. Much of the federal grassland in this area is rented to ranchers to graze cattle, sheep, and bison. In some places, erosion has worn the soft sandstone earth into bizarrely shaped cliffs, buttes, pillars, and gorges—creating a type of landscape called Badlands.

South Dakota's Geographical Features

Total area; rank	77,121 sq. mi. (199,743 sq km); 17th
Land; rank	75,897 sq. mi. (196,573 sq km); 16th
Water; rank	1,225 sq. mi. (3,173 sq km); 24th
***Inland water*; rank**	1,225 sq. mi. (3,173 sq km); 16th
Geographic center	Hughes, 8 miles (13 km) northeast of Pierre
Highest point	Harney Peak, 7,242 feet (2,208 m)
Lowest point	Big Stone Lake, 962 feet (293 m)
Largest city	Sioux Falls
Population; rank	699,999 (1990 census); 45th
Record high temperature	120°F (49°C) at Gannvalley on July 5, 1936
Record low temperature	–58°F (–50°C) at McIntosh on February 17, 1936
Average July temperature	74°F (23°C)
Average January temperature	16°F (–9°C)
Average annual precipitation	18 inches (46 cm)

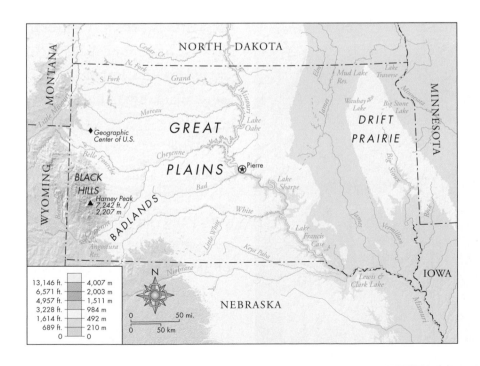

Topographical map
of South Dakota

The Black Hills rise at the western prairie edge. Thick forests of Black Hills spruce and ponderosa pine cover these granite hills and, from a distance, make them look black. The hills vary from rugged mountain terrain to soft, rolling meadows. Harney Peak at 7,242 feet (2,207 m) is the highest point between the Rocky Mountains and the European Alps. Two of the most dramatic and longest limestone caves in the world, Wind Cave and Jewel Cave, are found there.

From marshes to Badlands, from plains to peaks, South Dakota is full of natural riches. It's no wonder that one of the state's nicknames is the Land of Infinite Variety.

A fire lookout in the Black Hills

The Sacred Black Hills

The Black Hills of South Dakota have long been held sacred by the Native Americans. Black Elk, a Lakota holy man (1863–1950), said of Harney Peak, "There, when I was young, the spirits took me in my vision to the center of the earth and showed me all the good things in the sacred hoop of the world."

In Black Elk's day, Native Americans went to the Black Hills to pray and to renew mind and spirit. Today, Native Americans, residents, and visitors still experience that sense of renewal. They discover it as they drive the curving roads of the forests and Custer State Park or watch the sun turn the mountain walls pink with alpenglow. They feel it as they pass herds of bison grazing by the side of the road or watch eagles and owls in the evening sky. And they soon understand why the Black Hills are sacred to so many.

Parks, Forests, and Monuments

Although the entire state is magnificent—and don't try to tell any South Dakotan otherwise—the West is a treasure trove of natural beauty. The two most famous parks in South Dakota are there: Mount Rushmore National Memorial and Custer State Park. The Crazy Horse Memorial, a privately funded, nonprofit memorial, is also located there. The state has a total of nine national lands and six national wildlife refuges. It also manages twelve state parks, eighty-one state recreation areas, three state nature areas, and forty-four lakeside areas.

Granite needles in Custer State Park

Peter Norbeck

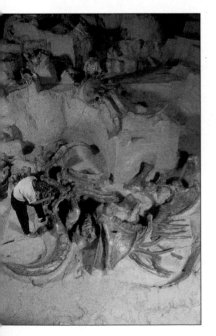

Peter Norbeck, who served as governor and U.S. senator, was one of South Dakota's greatest supporters. Through his efforts, the 73,000-acre (29,565-ha) Custer State Park was established in 1919.

Norbeck loved Doane Robinson's idea of having mountain sculptures in South Dakota, and used his influence to get the sculptor Gutzon Borglum involved. Norbeck, Robinson, and Borglum developed the design for the famous carving that became known as the Shrine of Democracy at Mount Rushmore. At Norbeck's urging, President Calvin Coolidge visited the Rushmore project. Coolidge liked the Black Hills area so much that he set up a summer White House in Custer Park and an office at the Rapid City High School. He pledged government support and money for completion of the sculpture.

Norbeck himself designed the twisting Iron Mountain Road, a scenic mountain road with tunnel views of Mount Rushmore. When engineers objected to the design, Norbeck proclaimed, "It's a scenic road. To do the scenery half-justice, people should drive 20 mph or under; to do it full justice, they should get out and walk!" ■

Clues to the Past

Deep in South Dakota's fossil-rich ground lies much information about America's ancient history. Throughout the state, scientists and amateurs hunt for signs of past animal and human life.

In 1990, Sue Henrickson found the world's largest and most complete *Tyrannosaurus rex* skeleton on a ranch in north-central South Dakota. Scientists named the dinosaur "Sue." In 1997, the Chicago Field Museum bought Sue at auction for $8.36 million. Museum experts have restored the skeleton and are now exhibiting it. In western South Dakota, scientists are unearthing other prehistoric animal skeletons, such as those of mammoths and giant sea turtles. The discovery of Sue raised many concerns about the ownership of fossils and the preservation of historical sites—issues that are still being discussed in South Dakota.

Remains of "Sue," the dinosaur

Badlands National Park

Southeast of the Black Hills are the Badlands, among the strangest landscapes found in the United States. Although it sounds like a hiding place for Hollywood bad guys, the area actually got its name from the Lakota Sioux, who called it *mako sica*, meaning "land bad." Later, trappers and settlers described the area as "bad lands" to travel across.

In 1939, a C-shaped portion of the extensive Badlands area was established as the Badlands National Monument. In 1978, it became a 244,000-acre (98,820-ha) national park. The park has three main areas: the Stronghold Unit and the Palmer Creek Unit—both within the Pine Ridge Indian Reservation—and the Sage Creek Wilderness Area. Today these are great lands to explore, with their odd shapes, bands of colors, sur-prising abundance of animal life, fossil history, and good roads and hiking trails.

Seventy-five million years ago, a warm shallow sea covered the Badlands. When the land rose and the water drained away, the sedimentary remains of that sea compressed into soft shale rock. Many plants and creatures died and sank to the seafloor, making this Pierre Shale Rock incredibly rich in fossils. Over the last 37 million years, wind and water have worn away portions of the shale leaving bizarre shapes including columns, bridges, and windows in the rock walls. The rock is actually very fragile and crumbles easily. Nature has not finished sculpting the Badlands. In half a million years, they will be gone, worn into a flat prairie.■

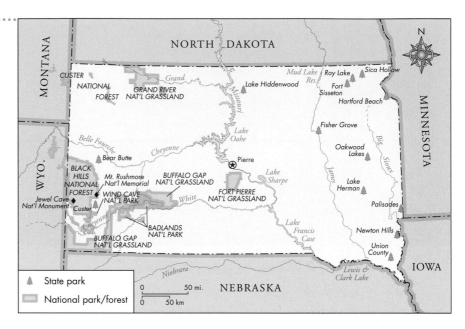

The pronghorn
antelope is among the
animals that are native
to South Dakota.

Scientists have discovered evidence from other time periods, too. In Mitchell, an ancient Indian village is being excavated and re-created. In Fort Pierre, archaeologists are uncovering the site of an early trading center. A 2,000-year-old site in the Badlands reveals how Indians living there once forced bison into a corral and killed them with spears.

Prairie Dogs and Friends

South Dakota may be best known for its bison and prairie dogs—but many other animals also live there, including mountain goats, bighorn sheep, pronghorn antelope, elk, white-tailed and mule deer, bobcats, porcupines, rabbits, mice, chipmunks, bats, and the ever-present coyote. Wild burros, descendants of those that escaped captivity during the gold-mining days, roam the Black Hills. Wild horses have long run free in the Badlands and a sanctuary near Hot Springs. South Dakota also has its share of snakes, including rattlesnakes and bull snakes.

Buffalo or Bison?

Actually, the name is *bison*. The buffalo is an African and Asian animal related to the ox. American bison is the correct name for the shaggy animal that we often call a "buffalo."

Bison are America's largest land animal. Males grow to be 6 feet (2 m) high and 9 to 12 feet (3 to 4 m) long. They live about thirty years. Although these animals weigh as much as 2,500 pounds (1,135 kg), they can run as fast as 32 miles (51 km) per hour. Female bison are smaller and lighter-colored. They give birth to one calf each spring.

Although bison are sociable with one another, they can be quick-tempered and fast to charge at people.

By the end of the early nineteenth century, bison were almost extinct. A man named Scotty Philip rounded up fifty-seven bison that he found living along the Cheyenne River in South Dakota, fenced them in, and protected them. Most modern-day herds come from those few animals. Today, more than 20,000 bison live in preserves and national parks in the United States, including 8,000 in South Dakota. ■

South Dakotans know well the sound of birds in the morning. More than 250 species of birds make their home in the state, including pheasant, turkeys, hawks, vultures, eagles, and pelicans. Shorebirds crowd the lakes and riverbanks; woodpeckers and songbirds fill the forest. Capitol Lake in Pierre is a stopover for thousands of migrating ducks and geese. South Dakota and the Missouri River are on the Central Flyway migration route, and millions of birds pass through the state each spring and fall, including whooping cranes, sandhill cranes, bald eagles, and trumpeter swans.

Prairie Grass, Pine Trees, and More

When people think of South Dakota's plant life, two things come to mind: prairie grass and the ponderosa pines of the Black Hills.

Prairie grass in evening light

Aspens in the Black Hills

These may be the most famous plants in the state, but there are many other types of vegetation too.

The prairie grass is a combination of more than fifty varieties of tall and short grasses and wildflowers. Big bluestem grass grows to 6 feet (2 m) tall and varies in color from bronze to steel blue, ripening to reds, browns, and purples. Other tall grasses include green needle grass, whose seeds have needlelike protrusions, and purple switchgrass. Western wheatgrass grows in mixed prairies, often with buffalo grass. The 5-inch (13-cm)-tall, gray-green buffalo grass is drought resistant. In drier areas, the Plains prickly pear cactus grows among the grasses.

Many varieties of wildflowers add color to the prairies. South Dakota's state flower, the American pasqueflower, a type of buttercup, grows 6 to 16 inches (15 to 41 centimeters) high and has white, blue, and lavender blooms. The tufted evening primrose has large flowers that bloom white in the evening, turn pink, and wilt by noon of the next day. Native Americans made soap from the root of the soapweed, a type of yucca, and ate the bulbs of the sego lily.

Forest covers about 4 percent of South Dakota. Alongside the dark ponderosa pine and Black Hills spruce trees grow aspen and juniper. In more arid areas such as the Badlands, eastern red cedar, Plains cottonwood, yellow willow, and the American elm also grow. Ash, oak, and willow are found along riverbanks throughout the state.

Rivers and Lakes

People think of South Dakota as dry prairie land, but the state is blessed with many rivers, lakes, and marshes. Several large rivers flow through the state: the Missouri, James, Cheyenne, Grand, Big Sioux, Moreau, Vermillion, Bad, and White. The building of dams on the Missouri River, completed in 1966, created 900 square miles (2,331 sq km) of reservoir lakes and 3,000 miles (4,827 km) of shoreline—wonderful areas for wildlife and recreation.

Lake Sylvan is located in Custer State Park.

Plains and Prairies

What is the difference between a plain and a prairie? Actually, both words can describe the same land area. The word *plain* describes the geological shape of the land—a large, flat area, often with limited rainfall. *Prairie* refers to the type of vegetation on the land—usually, a combination of meadow grasses and wildflowers. Even after plowing under the prairie grasses to create farmland, people in South Dakota continue to call the area a "prairie." ■

The eastern border of South Dakota resembles Minnesota with its many small lakes. One of the state's most beautiful lakes is Sylvan Lake in Custer State Park.

Sun, Wind, Rain, and Snow

South Dakota has four distinct seasons, all with comfortably low humidity. Lush, warm spring days, with their nourishing rains, lead to hot, sunny summers. Autumn brings warm days and crisp nights. When winter comes, it brings cold temperatures often with sunny days and clear nights. However, those beautiful winter days can also be stormy; the summer, hot and muggy; the fall, rainy and dreary; and spring, cool and soggy.

No matter what the season, the wind in South Dakota seems always to blow from the north and west. Sometimes, it is a welcome, cooling breeze. Other times, it is a frigid jolt or a dangerous storm. To break the winds and prevent topsoil from blowing away, most houses, pastures, and fields are bordered on the wind side by a stand of tall trees. Nothing stops tornadoes, though—and while most tornadoes quickly disappear, South Dakota has seen some of the worst. Most tornadoes occur in East River, which is in the part of the United States that gets four to six tornadoes per 10,000 square miles (25,900 sq km) each year.

Average January temperatures in the state range from 22°F (−6°C) in the southwest to 10°F (−13°C) in the northeast. Summer averages are 69°F (21°C) in the Black Hills and 79°F (26°C) in the eastern lowlands. The year of extreme temperatures was 1936. On February 17, it hit −58°F (−50°C) at McIntosh and that summer on July 5, it hit 120°F (49°C) at Gannvalley, only 150 miles (241 km) away.

Rapid City, in the west, has drier, less extreme weather than Sioux Falls, which is in the east. The eastern part of the state gets about 25 inches (64 cm) of precipitation, but regions west of the Missouri average 17 inches (43 cm). Although South Dakota has a reputation for winter blizzards, 80 to 90 percent of the precipitation falls as rain. Occasionally, that rain comes during summer thunderstorms, accompanied by hail the size of softballs.

Usually, South Dakota lives up to its nickname, the Sunshine State. But it has another nickname—the Blizzard State. Each year, the state budgets $5 million to remove snow and ice from the main roads. Some years, however, the snowstorms ignore the budget. During the winter of 1996–1997, for example, it snowed so much that it cost nearly $16 million to keep the roads clear. Still, many South Dakotans love the brisk feeling and fresh smell of snow on the wind.

A blizzard on a South Dakota prairie

CHAPTER SIX

Traveling South Dakota

Fields of corn are common sights in South Dakota.

Travelers crossing the northern United States pass through South Dakota on Interstate 90. They may even spend a night in Rapid City or Sioux Falls. As they speed across the central portion of the state, they may see dark hills against a blue sky in the west and the spiral shapes of the Badlands in the south. They will surely notice the rolling grasslands to the north and the pothole lakes and marshes to the east. These travelers may then believe they have seen South Dakota—but they don't know how much they have missed.

The Southeast

The southeastern portion of South Dakota is farming country, and corn grows as far as the eye can see. Pioneer towns, such as Sioux Falls, Yankton, and Vermillion, supported the early farms. Many of these towns are on rivers, which made it possible for farmers to harness water power for milling and for transporting grains.

Vermillion, named for the red-clay bluffs above the Vermillion River, is home to the University of South Dakota. One of the several museums on campus is the Shrine to Music Museum. Arne Larson, a music teacher, donated his collection of unique musical instruments to the university when he died. The collection has grown to include more than 6,000 rare and antique instruments—

Opposite: Fort Sisseton Cavalry

The Shrine to Music Museum in Vermillion

Highways and Byways

There are 83,376 miles (134,152 km) of roads and streets in South Dakota and 4,140 bridges. Two major interstate highways cross the state—Interstate 90 runs east and west, and Interstate 29 runs north and south. In 1995, vehicles traveled more than 7.7 billion miles (12.4 billion km) miles on those roads. Ten percent of the main roads and highways carried 66 percent of all that traffic. ■

including ivory lutes, Civil War band instruments, Persian drums, and one of only two Stradivari guitars in the world.

Near Vermillion is Spirit Mound dating back 10,000 years. It is one of the mysterious mounds thought to be Indian burial grounds. Native Americans told the nineteenth-century explorers Lewis and Clark that the mound was inhabited by small spirit warriors. Lewis and Clark climbed the mound and reported seeing a wonderful view of the prairie.

Upriver is the territorial capital, Yankton, and beyond that is the Lewis and Clark Recreational Area. During the summer, about 40,000 people each week enjoy camping, waterskiing, sailing, and other recreational activities at this reservoir lake.

Sioux Falls, which had 100,814 people in the 1990 census, is the largest city in South Dakota. The city stands alongside a series of red quartzite waterfalls on the Big Sioux River. The pretty town has tree-lined streets and more than sixty parks. It also has a modern mall and a charming historical shopping district. The Wash-

Following Lewis and Clark

When Lewis and Clark came to South Dakota in 1804, they paddled up the Missouri River. Travelers today can drive along the same river trail that these famous explorers followed.

At rest stops along the way, posted stories tell of the experiences of the Corps of Discovery expedition in South Dakota. The Lewis and Clark National Historic Trail is approximately 3,700 miles (5,953 km) long and passes through ten states. The Lewis and Clark Visitors Center is located at Gavins Point Dam in Nebraska, not far from Yankton. Exhibits also tell the history of the area. ■

ington Pavilion of Arts and Science, which opened in 1999, attracts top entertainers.

Since statehood, Sioux Falls has been a center of commerce and industry, processing and transporting farm and animal products. Today, it is a growing financial center. One of the nation's largest banks and a major computer company have offices there. Sioux Falls has low crime, low unemployment, and many medical facil-

A Sioux Falls neighborhood

ities. It also has a great zoo and offers all sorts of other fun activities—from golf to rodeo.

Just north of Sioux Falls and Palisades State Park is Devil's Gulch. According to legend, the outlaw Jesse James came to this gulch while he was being chased by a posse after a bank robbery. The posse was glad to have him finally trapped—but James had another idea. He and his horse took a running jump and cleared the 20-foot (6-m)-wide and 50-foot (15-m)-deep crevice. Today, there's a footbridge across the gulch.

West of Sioux Falls is Mitchell, a town that takes corn seriously. One of the oddest buildings in South Dakota—or anywhere else for that matter—is the Mitchell Corn Palace. The building was created in 1892 for the Corn Belt Exposition. To call the attention of passersby to the exhibit, the outside of the build-

The Mitchell Corn Palace is a spectacle.

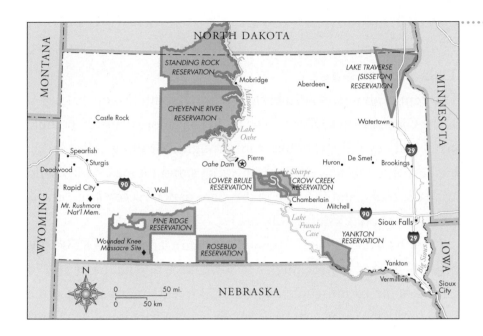

ing was decorated with various kinds of corn and grain. The reaction was so positive that the residents of Mitchell have continued the tradition since then.

Each September, during a weeklong festival, people decorate large panels on the exterior walls of the building and three interior walls with new murals and designs around a particular theme—for example, "Youth in Action" or "Building a Nation." As decoration, they use thousands of bushels of corn, grain, and grasses of all colors. Grasses, tied into bunches, and halved ears of corn are nailed onto the walls, according to an artist's design. For many years, famed Sioux artist Oscar Howe designed the murals. The project has cost as much as $100,000.

During the rest of the year, the Corn Palace hosts conventions, shows, and sporting events. Each year, more than 400,000 people from around the world come to visit the building and shop at the "corn-cessions" inside.

The Northeast

The gentle, abundant northeastern area of South Dakota is known as the Glacial Lakes District. The region has more than 120 pothole lakes and several rivers that run through its rolling hills. Trees, bushes, and wildflowers grow in valleys and ravines. Many wild animals, birds, and fish live in the state parks, recreational areas, and two national wildlife refuges.

South Dakota State University, the state's largest with 8,500 students, is located in Brookings. The town has a population of 16,270 and is home to museums and cultural events that are not often found in towns of its size. The university's agricultural programs have made Brookings the agricultural center of the state.

West of Brookings is the town of De Smet, one of the best-loved towns of America's children. Author Laura Ingalls Wilder grew up in De Smet and wrote about it in her *Little House* series of

The Ingalls Homestead site

books, which she began in 1932. The Wilder home is open for tours. Each summer, during a Laura Ingalls Wilder Festival, her stories are acted out and lectures given about her work and life. Many visitors come to the events wearing costumes.

Watertown, to the northeast, is a prairie community of about 17,592 people, with parks, trails, and nearby lakes. Uptown Watertown, the renovated historical district, is full of stores, antique shops, and art galleries. Artist Terry Redlin, whose prints of rural scenes sell nationwide, lives in Watertown, and the newly built Redlin Art Center showcases his work. Historical buildings open to the public include the Mellette House, home of South Dakota's first governor.

Arthur C. Mellette is dear to South Dakotans because of his sense of honor. After he left office, his friend, the state treasurer, embezzled, or stole, state funds. Mellette gave money from his personal fortune to repay the state for its losses. Just outside of town, sitting high atop a hill, is the modern Mother of God Monastery, home of the Benedictine Sisters. The white building, completed in 1997, has large windows on all sides and 45,000 square feet (4,185 sq m) of space.

North of Watertown lies Fort Sisseton, one of the best-preserved historical forts in the United States. It once housed as many as 400 soldiers. Each June, the Fort Sisseton Festival comes alive with bugle blowing, tomahawk throwing, fiddling, square dancing, and battle reenactments—although no battles were actually ever fought there.

To the west is Aberdeen, the state's third-largest city, with a population of 24,927. Aberdeen began as a hub on the railroad line. The president of the railroad named the settlement after his home in Aberdeen, Scotland. Visitors enjoy the Dacotah Prairie Museum, Northern State University, and Storybook Land, a park with exhibits from America's favorite stories. Its Emerald City exhibit is based on the book *The Wonderful Wizard of Oz*, written in 1900 by former Aberdeen resident L. Frank Baum.

Most of South Dakota's open prairie is now farmland, but 50

Arthur Mellette was South Dakota's first governor.

miles (80 km) northwest of Aberdeen lies the Samuel Ordway Prairie. This 7,600-acre (3,078-ha) plot of prairie grass, owned by the Nature Conservancy, looks just as it might have looked a millennium ago. Bison still graze on its windswept hills.

The Central Region

The Missouri River flows through the central region of the state, almost dividing it in two. According to Indian legend, the river burst forth when the Great Spirit split the land with a tomahawk. At the river, the land changes from the farmland of East River to the rolling grassland of West River. From the northern border to Pierre, the river serves as the dividing line between Mountain Time and Central Time.

Sitting Bull's grave

On the western shore of Lake Oahe are the Standing Rock and Cheyenne River Indian Reservations. Not far from Mobridge, on a bluff overlooking the Missouri River, is Sitting Bull's grave and memorial. After Sitting Bull's death in 1890, the army buried him at Fort Yates in North Dakota. In 1953, his descendants moved Sitting Bull's remains to the river bluff on the Standing Rock Reservation and reburied them in a cement vault.

South along the river stands Pierre, the capital of South Dakota. Pierre takes its name from the French fur trader Pierre Chouteau Jr. With a population of 13,000, Pierre is the second-smallest capital city in the United States. What it lacks in size, however, it makes up for with flair.

The grounds of the capitol, one of the loveliest spots in the state, has trails winding through sculpture-filled gardens and along Capitol Lake. The elegant building has sweeping views of the river and beyond. Built into a hillside near the capitol is the Cultural Heritage Center, whose exhibits tell the history of South Dakota. No wonder Pierre is considered one of the ten best small towns in the nation.

The capitol at Pierre is set in a pretty and peaceful area.

Near Chamberlain, Interstate 90 crosses the Missouri River. On the wooded bluff beside the river is a rest stop with a modernistic sculpture of a tepee. The rest area has a scenic view of the river— a good place to stop and wonder what the Indians and pioneers might have thought when they first saw the great river.

To the west, south of Interstate 90, are the Rosebud Indian Reservation, the Pine Ridge Indian Reservation, and Badlands

The Wall Drugstore

The town of Wall, named for its position on a cliff wall in the Badlands, has the most famous drugstore in the world. Pharmacist Ted Hustead and his wife, Dorothy, were having a hard time making ends meet during the Great Depression. One hot summer day, Dorothy watched as cars of people drove by, wondering how to get them to stop in the store and spend a bit of time and money. "Free ice water, of course!" she thought. Her husband made dozens of signs, indicating the number of miles to Wall Drugstore and free ice water, and posted them along the highway.

People have been talking about the signs and stopping at Wall Drugstore ever since. Today, signs throughout the world point the way to free ice water in Wall. The Husteads' store has grown to the length of the street. Although the building still has the original pharmacy, it now contains a museum, souvenir shop, bookstore, Western-wear store—and a large restaurant that still serves five-cent cups of coffee and thousands of glasses of free ice water on hot summer days. ■

National Park. This area has an incredible, stark beauty. Wide skies with scattered wisps of clouds turn turquoise, fuchsia, and gold at sunset and sunrise. Cattle, bison, and wild horses graze on the carved bluffs and the short grasses of the prairie land.

The reservations are open to visitors. The land looks much the same as it did when Native Americans hunted bison there long ago. Few fences divide the countryside, and no shopping-mall parking lots clutter the small towns. In the south-central part of the Pine Ridge Reservation is the Wounded Knee Memorial and Massacre Site. The Pine Ridge Indian Reservation is the nation's second-largest reservation after Arizona's Navajo Reservation. Because few good jobs are available, life on the reservations can be hard. Many people are forced to leave to find work in the cities. Shannon County, on the Pine Ridge Reservation, is the poorest county in America.

Native American elders dancing at sunset

The West

In western South Dakota, the prairie's edge meets the Black Hills. Little mountain towns are scattered through some of America's prettiest countryside. The Iron Mountain and Needles Highways twist through narrow canyons and around granite cathedral spires. Built in the days of the Great Depression, these narrow roads were not made for modern traffic. They are so treacherous that they close for the winter season and become snowmobile trails. Other popular activities in the region include rock climbing, horseback riding, and fishing in the clear mountain streams. The weather is moderate, and the mountains offer some protection from the wind.

Rapid City, the second-largest city in South Dakota, is on the eastern edge of the hills, by the rapids of Rapid Creek. Although it's a small city of 54,523, Rapid City is full of interesting things to see and do.

The Journey Museum, with its high-tech exhibits, retraces 2.5 billion years of South Dakota's history. The Museum of Geology houses dinosaur bones, and Dinosaur Park has life-size concrete dinosaurs. Memorial Park contains a piece of the Berlin Wall, a symbol of communist oppression and now a symbol of peace in Europe. Stavkirke—the Chapel in the Hills—is an exact replica of an 850-year-old church in Norway, built in honor of European traditions and heritage. Near the Ellsworth Air Force Base is the Air and Space Museum, which has a collection of bombers, missiles, and planes from the early days of flight through the years of the Cold War between the United States and the Soviet Union (1945–1991).

South of Rapid City are two world-famous monuments: Mount Rushmore and the Crazy Horse Memorial. At nearby Custer State

Stavkirke

Park, visitors on the wildlife-loop road are certain to see bison—and possibly wild burros, antelope, deer, elk, or bighorn sheep. Even without the wildlife, the spectacular lakes and mountains make any visit a pleasure. Movies, television shows, and commercials that need a dramatic Western backdrop are often filmed in the park.

South and west of Custer State Park are Jewel Cave and Wind Cave National Parks. The walls of Jewel Cave have jewel-like crystal formations. It is the second-longest cave in the United States, with at least 110 miles (177 km) of passages. Wind Cave is 81 miles (130 km) long, and its walls are covered with unique formations that resemble boxes, popcorn, and frost. National park rangers give guided tours of both caves.

Many of the small mountain towns west of Rapid City—in what was once gold-rush country—have become popular tourism and recreation spots. Deadwood, which has a population of 2,000, recently capitalized on its history as a gambling town. In 1989, it legalized gambling and restored the town to its appearance during the late nineteenth century—except for the nearby parking garage.

Deadwood is now a tourist attraction.

Today, Deadwood is a popular destination for tourists who want to relive the good old days of the gold rush.

Nearby Spearfish is a recreation area. Spearfish Canyon is great for biking, hiking, horseback riding, and, in winter, cross-country skiing. The D. C. Booth Historic National Fish Hatchery has been operating since 1899, ensuring good fishing in the area. For more than sixty years, local actors have performed the Black Hills Passion Play for summer visitors in the outdoor amphitheater.

Each August, the little town of Sturgis, population 6,000, fills with hundreds of thousands of people as motorcyclists arrive for the Sturgis Rally and Races. People come to attend workshops, talk with vendors, and attend the races, concerts, and parties—but mostly they come to see all the other bikes and the bikers. The festival has even become a popular spot for motorcycle enthusiasts to marry.

North of Sturgis, along Highway 85 and just 17 miles (27 km) from Castle Rock, is the Center of the Nation marker. South Dakota is, indeed, in the middle of everywhere.

CHAPTER SEVEN

The Shape of Government

South Dakotans believe in independence and self-reliance. These strong values color everything they do, including how they shape their government.

The capitol grounds are known for their sculptures, design, and beauty.

Like most U.S. states, South Dakota has a three-branch government: executive, legislative, and judicial. These branches were established by the state constitution, which was adopted just before statehood in 1889. The constitution has been changed, or amended, eighty times.

One of the most important changes was made to allow an individual citizen to present a particular concern to other citizens for a vote. Today, if a South Dakotan wants a law passed or revoked, the person can write what is called an initiative. If 5 percent of all the people who voted in the last election for governor sign a petition to support it, the initiative is put on the ballot. If the citizens of South Dakota vote for the initiative, it becomes law. South Dakota was the first state in the nation to adopt this initiative process.

Opposite: The state capitol

South Dakotans like to have their say. The percentage of citizens who vote in South Dakota is much higher than the percentage in most other states. They know their vote counts, and they take the responsibility of voting seriously. Because South Dakota's population is small, voters have a good chance to meet the candidates and become informed about the issues. On both state and local levels, many government positions are filled through voting; in other states, the governor or mayor may appoint people to fill those same positions.

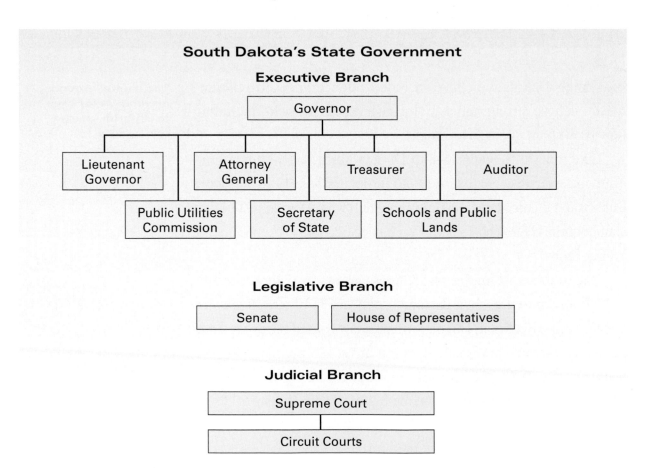

South Dakota's State Government

Executive Branch

Governor

Lieutenant Governor | Attorney General | Treasurer | Auditor

Public Utilities Commission | Secretary of State | Schools and Public Lands

Legislative Branch

Senate | House of Representatives

Judicial Branch

Supreme Court

Circuit Courts

The Three Branches

The executive branch consists of the governor, lieutenant governor, secretary of state, attorney general, and several commissioners. All are elected to four-year terms. The governor, lieutenant governor, and other high-ranking officials may serve only two consecutive terms. After Governor William Janklow served two terms, from 1979–1987, he took eight years off before being elected to a third and fourth term. If the governor wants to serve another term, he must take another period of time off.

The legislative branch has two houses: the senate and the house of representatives. The senate has thirty-five members; the house of representatives has seventy. Members of both serve two-year terms and may not serve more than four consecutive

South Dakota's Governors

Name	Party	Term	Name	Party	Term
Arthur C. Mellette	Rep.	1889–1893	Harlan J. Bushfield	Rep.	1939–1943
Charles H. Sheldon	Rep.	1893–1897	M. Q. Sharpe	Rep.	1943–1947
Andrew E. Lee	Populist	1897–1901	George T. Mickelson	Rep.	1947–1951
Charles N. Herreid	Rep.	1901–1905	Sigurd Anderson	Rep.	1951–1955
Samuel H. Elrod	Rep.	1905–1907	Joseph J. Foss	Rep.	1955–1959
Coe I. Crawford	Rep.	1907–1909	Ralph Herseth	Dem.	1959–1961
Robert S. Vessey	Rep.	1909–1913	Archie Gubbrud	Rep.	1961–1965
Frank M. Byrne	Rep.	1913–1917	Nils Boe	Rep.	1965–1969
Peter Norbeck	Rep.	1917–1921	Frank L. Farrar	Rep.	1969–1971
W. H. McMaster	Rep.	1921–1925	Richard F. Kneip	Dem.	1971–1978
Carl Gunderson	Rep.	1925–1927	Harvey L. Wollman	Dem.	1978–1979
W. J. Bulow	Dem.	1927–1931	William J. Janklow	Rep.	1979–1987
Warren Green	Rep.	1931–1933	George S. Mickelson	Rep.	1987–1993
Thomas "Tom" Berry	Dem.	1933–1937	Walter Dale Miller	Rep.	1993–1995
Leslie Jensen	Rep.	1937–1939	William J. Janklow	Rep.	1995–

High school students watching the state Senate from the gallery

terms. Legislators are elected from South Dakota's thirty-five districts. To keep the population evenly distributed among the districts, the boundaries of the districts are redrawn every ten years if necessary.

South Dakota's counties

The legislative session begins on the second Tuesday of January at noon. In odd-numbered years, the session lasts forty days; in even-numbered years, it lasts only thirty-five days. If emergency issues arise, either the governor or the legislature can call a special session. Because the regular session is short, representatives are less likely to become professional politicians; instead, they remain citizens representing their neighbors.

The judicial branch consists of a five-member state supreme court and seven circuit courts served by thirty-six judges. Counties and cities also have their own lower courts.

South Dakota's supreme court

The Capitol

The state capitol in Pierre is one of the most beautiful and accessible state capitols in the United States. The white marble and limestone building stands on a gentle hill above the Missouri River, surrounded by a 5-acre (2-ha) lake and 115 acres (47 ha) of gardens, trails, and statues. The 161-foot (49-m) dome is covered with 40,000 pounds (18,160 kg) of copper. Inside, an inner dome of stained glass rises 96 feet (29 m) above the mosaic floor.

A grand staircase leads from the rotunda entryway to the chambers of the senate and house of representatives. Murals, stained-glass windows, intricately carved wood panels, paintings, sculptures, and bronze castings decorate the building.

All the flags that have flown over what is now South Dakota are displayed in the rotunda. They include a Sioux chief's staff, the French flag, the Spanish flag, the Dakota Territory flag, the state flag, and the U.S. flag.

Within the rotunda are symbols and colors representing Native Americans' seven sacred directions: north, east, south, west, up, down, and center. A white flag represents the north, the direction from which snow comes; a yellow flag stands for the east, the direction of the rising sun; a red flag, for the south, the direction from which the sun shines; and a black flag, for the west, the direction from which thunder comes. The floor's green terrazzo tiles represent the grass of the earth below, and, above, blue stained glass represents the sky. According to Indian beliefs, the seventh direction is the direction of the spirit at the center of each of us. This direction is represented by a brass triangle in the center of the rotunda floor. This also symbolizes that people are at the center of South Dakota's government.

The capitol's floor is inlaid with millions of handmade inch-square tiles. Sixty-six Italian artists laid out the intricate floor designs. To sign their work, they each put a blue tile, called a signature stone, somewhere in the floor. After almost 100 years, only fifty-five of the sixty-six stones have been found.

As South Dakota approached its centennial celebration in 1989, a massive renovation of the capitol took place. South Dakotans are proud of the work done to bring this building back to its original glory. ■

Unlike the borders of the legislative districts, the borders of the state's sixty-six counties and six reservations are permanent. They also have their own governments. The counties are governed by a three-to-five-member commission whose members are elected for four-year terms. South Dakotans elect more local government officials than most states, including the state attorney, county auditor, registrar of deeds, coroner, sheriff, and treasurer. The 1934 Indian Reorganization Act gave Native American reservations the oppor-

Senator Tom Daschle

Tom Daschle grew up in Aberdeen, the eldest of four boys. He enjoyed tennis, drawing, hunting, and reading—especially history books. His parents worked hard to create a good life for their children. Tom helped out by working on his uncle's farm and running a concession stand with his best friend.

As a teenager, Tom listened to President John F. Kennedy's speeches, in which he spoke about ideals, commitment, and service to the country. As Kennedy spoke, Tom clearly saw the direction that his life would take—he would enter public service. He started immediately, as his high school's class president.

He attended South Dakota State University majoring in political science and became the first college graduate in his family. After serving in the U.S. Air Force, Tom pursued his dream of entering politics.

In 1978, he ran for the U.S. House of Representatives and won by only 139 votes. In 1986, he ran for the Senate and won by 52 percent; in 1998, he won

again, by 62 percent. Senator Daschle works hard for the special concerns of his constituents—farming issues, veterans affairs, health care, and education.

Because of his reputation for helping people to reach agreement, Tom quickly became a Senate leader. When nominating him for the top Senate Democratic leadership position, Senator Robert Byrd said, "He has steel in his spine despite his reasonable and modest demeanor." Senator Daschle says his South Dakota upbringing taught him to value family and hard work, instilled in him a love of nature and community, and gave him a good education. ■

Governor William Janklow

When William Janklow was a teenager, no one could have predicted that he would become a lawyer like his father—or a popular, four-term governor. Janklow's father was a prosecutor at the Nuremberg Trials, in which war criminals were tried after World War II. He died when William was still a child, and the family then moved from Chicago, Illinois, to Flandreau, South Dakota—the town where William's mother grew up. At sixteen years of age, William dropped out of school and dropped into trouble. Eventually, a judge gave him a choice: join the military or spend time in juvenile hall.

The young man joined the U.S. Marines and quickly learned how he wanted to spend his future. After leaving the Marines, he enrolled at the University of South Dakota. In the middle of the semester, however, school officials discovered that he had never graduated from high school. They wanted to force him to leave the university. The clever future lawyer made a deal with them: If his first-semester grades were good enough, they would let him stay. Soon, William had graduated from the university and law school.

Attorney Janklow began his career as a legal-aid lawyer on the Rosebud Indian Reservation. He later was elected attorney general and eventually became governor. Today, Governor Janklow continues to work for lower taxes, greater efficiency in state government, the encouragement of new businesses, reform of the prison system, increased tourism, and the best education possible for South Dakota's children. ■

tunity to form their own tribal governments and establish their own police forces.

Like all states, South Dakota sends two senators to Washington, D.C., but, because of its low population, the state has only one representative. For many years, the state voted almost consistently Republican but since the election of a Democratic governor in 1958, there has been representation by both major parties.

Outstanding Women of South Dakota

Gertrude Simmons Bonnin, or Zitkala-Sa, was a Yankton Dakota Sioux born in 1876—a time when neither Indians nor women had much power or influence. But that didn't stop her. Her talents as a teacher, musician, writer, and lecturer led her from South Dakota to Washington, D.C., where she became an outspoken and influential activist for Indian rights. In 1921, Bonnin formed the National Council of American Indians and worked to improve conditions for Native Americans.

Carole Hillard is a teacher who became an activist and a politician.

In 1995, she was elected the first female lieutenant governor of South Dakota. From 1991 to 1994, she served in the state's house of representatives. She also served on many public-service boards and committees—including Rapid City's Big Brothers/Big Sisters Organization. As lieutenant governor, her primary concerns are child care and the welfare of the elderly. She has received the Governor's Outstanding Citizen Award, and in 1993, was named one of South Dakota's outstanding women. These are two of many special South Dakota women. ■

Political Leaders

For a state with such a small population, South Dakota has contributed many leaders to national politics, including Vice President Hubert Humphrey and presidential candidate Senator George McGovern. Joe Foss, a World War II pilot and hero, served both as governor and U.S. senator. Ben Reifel, who was born on the Rosebud Indian Reservation and received a doctoral degree from Harvard University, became an influential U.S. congressman. Tom Daschle, one of South Dakota's current senators, is helping guide the future path of the nation as Senate minority leader.

South Dakota's State Flag and Seal

South Dakota has two official flags. The 1909 flag had two sides, with the state seal on one side and the sun on the other. Because it was expensive to manufacture a double-sided flag, a second design was adopted in 1963, and updated in 1992. The state's blue flag now shows the state seal surrounded by a sunburst and the words "South Dakota" and "The Mount Rushmore State," which is the state's official nickname.

The state seal of South Dakota, adopted in 1889, contains symbols of several important industries and resources. Agriculture is represented by a farmer plowing a field of corn; ranching, by cattle on the grasslands; and mining, by a smelting furnace. At the center of the seal, as in the center of the state, a riverboat steams along the Missouri River. At the top of the seal is the state motto, "Under God, the people rule." ∎

South Dakota's State Song

Hail! South Dakota

The words and music to South Dakota's state song, "Hail, South Dakota," were written by Deecort Hammitt. This marching song officially became the state song in 1943.

Hail! South Dakota, A great state
    of the land,
Health, wealth and beauty, That's
    what makes her grand;
She has her Black Hills, And
    mines with gold so rare,
And with her scenery, No other
    state can compare.

Come where the sun shines, And
    where life's worth your while,
You won't be here long, 'Till you'll
    wear a smile;
No state's so healthy, And no folk
    quite so true,

To South Dakota. We welcome
    you.

Hail! South Dakota, The state we
    love the best,
Land of our fathers, Builders of
    the west;
Home of the Badlands, and Rush-
    more's ageless shrine,
Black Hills and prairies, Farmland
    and Sunshine.
Hills, farms and prairies, Blessed
    with bright Sunshine.

South Dakota's State Symbols

State flower: American pasqueflower Adopted in 1903, this purple wildflower (top right) grows throughout the state. Its blossoms signal that spring has arrived.

State tree: Black Hills spruce The Black Hills are covered with these evergreen trees. From a distance, their dark, blue-green color looks black, giving the hills their name. The Black Hills spruce was adopted in 1947.

State bird: Ring-necked pheasant This beautiful bird (center right) was brought into the state as a game bird in 1898 and has thrived here ever since. It became the state bird in 1943.

State animal: Coyote The coyote is found throughout the state, especially in the river valleys and the Black Hills. These animals help control the rodent population. The coyote was adopted as the state animal in 1949.

State fish: Walleye Adopted in 1982, the walleye is a popular game fish found in lakes and the Missouri River. The largest walleye on record weighed 15 pounds 3 ounces (7 kg).

State grass: Western wheatgrass This grass, adopted in 1970, is grown mostly as feed for livestock.

State insect: Honeybee The light, high-quality honey of this pollinating insect is an important product of South Dakota. The honeybee was adopted as the state insect in 1978.

State fossil: *Triceratops* This dinosaur lived in western South Dakota 68 million years ago.

State mineral: Rose quartz This pink stone (bottom right), adopted as the state mineral in 1966, is found in the southern Black Hills. It sometimes has veins of gold. Rose quartz is used for jewelry and other decorative objects.

State gemstone: Fairburn agate Adopted in 1966, this banded agate is a favorite gemstone for jewelry and rock collections.

State soil: Houdek This deep, well-drained, loamy soil is one of South Dakota's most valuable resources. It was named the state soil in 1990.

State drink: Milk Adopted in 1986, milk is the official drink of South Dakota, reflecting the importance of the state's dairy industry.

State musical instrument: Fiddle The fiddle, which has been a popular musical instrument in South Dakota since pioneer days, was adopted as the state instrument in 1989.

CHAPTER EIGHT

Cattle, Corn, and Computers

Farms dominate the land in South Dakota.

Cattle, corn, computers, credit cards—and the many visitors that come to the state to see the sights—all help South Dakotans make a living. In the past, the state's economy has swung up and down with farm prices—boom or bust. Those bust times have come all too often for South Dakotans. The state has worked hard to help its citizens and keep the economy stable by making sure people can always make a good living.

State leaders have passed laws to attract new businesses to South Dakota, bringing more jobs and a more diverse economy. The Small Business Survival Index ranked South Dakota as the best

Opposite: A cattle roundup

Why Farm Prices Rise and Fall

What farmers get paid for their farm products vary with supply and demand—how much is available and how much customers want to buy. Prices are usually calculated each week, based on the answers to these questions:

1. How much of the product has been produced? The amount may vary, depending on how much land has been planted, the type of seed used, and weather conditions. Good growing conditions create what are called "bumper crops."

2. How much of the product has been saved from previous years? For example, many crops are kept in storage and sold gradually over time.

3. How much of the product is available elsewhere? If there is a great supply of a crop everywhere, for example, the price falls. If the crop has failed in other areas, the price rises because there is less to buy. A South Dakotan farmer once said about farming, "It's a sorry way to make a living, to profit from someone else's misfortune."

4. How much is the buyer's money worth? Because South Dakota's products are sold throughout the world, the prices of foreign currency also have a big influence. For example, when the Japanese yen was strong, 90 yen bought a dollar's worth of grain. When Japan had a banking crisis, the economy and the yen weakened. Then, it cost 130 yen to buy a dollar's worth of grain. The high price discouraged Japanese customers from buying. This created a surplus of the grain in the American market which, in turn, reduced the price paid to the farmer. ■

economic environment in the nation for entrepreneurs—people who start businesses. South Dakota has no personal income, property, business, or corporate tax. The state has thirty-four other types of taxes, however, such as sales, gambling, gas, and car-license taxes. Even with its low taxes, South Dakota has shown its prairie practicality by balancing its budget every year since statehood.

The Farming Community

When some people think of South Dakota, they think of farms—and they should. There are 32,500 farms in the state, averaging 1,354 acres (548 ha) each, for a total of 44 million acres (18 million ha) of farmland. About 90 percent of the state's land is used for farming or ranching.

Agriculture is big business in South Dakota. The top commodities are cattle, wheat, hogs, corn, and soybeans. Other important products are sunflowers for seed and oil, oats, rye, sorghum, dairy products, sheep and wool, and chickens and eggs. Farm products make up only 11 percent of South Dakota's gross state product, which is the total value of the work completed and the goods produced in the state. If the value of the many supporting agricultural businesses is added, however, the farming industry equals about 40 percent of the gross state product.

The computer industry has made a home in South Dakota.

The Business Community

There is more to South Dakota than its farms, however. Some of its towns, especially in East River, have become major financial and industrial centers. Sioux Falls is home to the national Citibank Corporation. Credit-card bills are sent from Sioux Falls to customers throughout the world. When Mutual of Omaha Insurance Company searched the nation to find the best place for its new

Ted Waitt

Ted Waitt grew up on his family's farm near Sioux City, Iowa—and so did his father, grandfather, and great-grandfather. The black-and-white spots of a Holstein cow were in his future—but those cows weren't on any farm.

In 1985, Waitt and a friend made their own makeshift computer, and soon Waitt was building computers for friends. Waitt was raised to believe that, with hard work, he could do anything—so he decided to start his own business, making and selling computers.

He began the business in his parents' barn on Gateway Road, but it was immediately so successful that he moved to large, new offices in Sioux Falls, South Dakota. Fourteen years later, Waitt's barn business had grown to a $7.5-billion-a-year business. The company has headquarters in South Dakota, California, Ireland, Australia, Japan, and Malaysia.

Remembering his beginnings in the barn, Waitt named his company Gateway. Gateway's black-and-white logo—which is also the design on the company's boxes—was inspired by the spots of the Holstein dairy cows on the Waitt family farm. ▪

health-care service center, it chose Aberdeen. A new $100-million regional railway center will soon be built near Huron. The computer company Gateway has offices in Sioux Falls and North Sioux City. Finance makes up about 21 percent of the gross state product.

The cost of living is lower in South Dakota than in large commercial centers, so businesses in the state are often able to pay lower wages and workers are able to live well on them. Part of their good lifestyle is an average commuting time for most workers of 14 minutes, far less than in most big cities.

Not only do businesses in South Dakota save on taxes and wages, they get some of the best workers in the nation. The values

Allen Neuharth

Growing up poor in South Dakota taught Allen Neuharth all about determination and hard work. It took just that for him to build one of the nation's most popular and best-known newspapers—*USA Today.*

When Al was very young, his father died. His mother worked many part-time jobs, and Al and his brother also worked to help support the family. Al's first job was a paper route that he started at age ten. The news business stayed with him. As a young man, he started a sports weekly in South Dakota. The paper didn't succeed, but he learned a great deal about success and failure.

With the help of those hard lessons, in 1970 he became president of the Gannett Company, a huge communication company. In 1982, his vision and determination led to the creation of *USA Today,* the country's first national, general-interest newspaper. *USA Today* has been called the "traveling American's newspaper" because of its national coverage and its appeal for people on the go. ■

of the early prairie farmers—hard work and honesty—are still strong in South Dakota. You show up on time, you do the job, and if the person next to you needs help, you help. In South Dakota, there is honor in a job well done. Ted Waitt, the president of Gateway, said, "Having worked in other areas of the country, I can attest to the remarkable difference in the attitude and aptitude of the South Dakota workforce."

Tourism

Tourism is big business in South Dakota. In 1998, 2.5 million visitors from around the world visited Mount Rushmore in the Black Hills. While there, many took side trips to visit the Crazy Horse Memorial; Custer State Park to see bison herds; Wild West towns,

such as Deadwood; the Black Hills cave district; the Badlands; and the Pine Ridge and Rosebud Indian Reservations.

In 1998, visitors to South Dakota brought $585 million into the state—an increase of 13.8 percent over 1997. Tourism is alive and well—and growing—in South Dakota, a state blessed with so many interesting things to see.

Manufacturing and Mining

From 1988 to 1998, South Dakota's manufacturing increased 56 percent, the second-highest growth rate in the nation. Nearly 50,000 people have jobs in manufacturing machinery, food products, scientific instruments, electronic equipment, lumber products, and publications. These industries produce more than $3 billion in goods.

South Dakota has been the nation's number-one gold producer since 1944. The Homestake Gold Mine in Lead is the richest and longest-producing mine in the United States. With the falling price of gold, however, the mine has cut back its production levels—but

Opposite: Visitors at the Mount Rushmore National Memorial

What South Dakota Grows, Manufactures, and Mines

Agriculture	Manufacturing	Mining
Beef cattle	Food products	Gold
Corn	Machinery	Petroleum
Hay	Electronic equipment	Clay
Hogs	Scientific instruments	Feldspar
Milk	Lumber products	Gravel
Soybeans		Limestone
Sunflowers		Granite
Wheat		

The Homestake Gold Mine has been operating since 1876.

the gold is still there, waiting for the day when prices will rise again.

South Dakota's other mining products include petroleum, clay, feldspar, gravel, sand, and stone—especially limestone and granite, which have become popular for floor tiles and countertops in homes. The state's sales of these stone products rose from $12 billion in 1990 to $26 billion in 1997.

Oahe Dam

Oahe Dam, just upriver from Pierre, was created as part of the Flood Control Act passed by Congress in 1944. It is one of four dams in South Dakota that help control flooding along the Missouri and Mississippi Rivers. Work began on the project in 1948. In 1962, President John F. Kennedy dedicated the dam.

Oahe Dam, which is 245 feet (75 m) high and 9,360 feet (2,855 m) long, is the second-largest rolled-earth dam in the world. Only the Aswan Dam in Egypt is larger. The dam holds back Lake Oahe, the fourth-largest reservoir lake in the United States. The lake extends 231 miles (372 km), all the way into North Dakota. It has a shoreline of 2,250 miles (3,620 km) and a maximum depth of 205 feet (63 m).

Water from the lake pours into seven, tall tornado turbines that sit on top of the dam. The turbines spin the water at 117 miles (188 km) per hour, creating electricity for South Dakota, North Dakota, Nebraska, Minnesota, and Montana. Then the water is released into the river through 140 wicket gates. At full capacity, 420,000 gallons (1.6 million liters) of water flow through the turbines every second.

If the river waters—anywhere from Montana to Louisiana—are high because of heavy rains, water is held in the lake to help avoid flooding. If water is needed downriver for irrigation, safe navigation, or other purposes, more water is released.

The Oahe Dam has spawned many new recreational businesses in the area, including a hatchery for Chinook salmon. Each year, more than 1.5 million visitors enjoy camping, boating, windsurfing, fishing, hunting, picnicking, and hiking on the nature trails all along the lake created by the dam. ■

Deviled Walleye Fillets

This devilishly delicious dinner is made from walleye fish, which are found in lakes and rivers throughout South Dakota. This popular game fish is also the state fish.

Ingredients:

- 1 small onion, finely diced
- 1/2 small green pepper, chopped
- 1/4 pound butter
- 3 tablespoons lemon juice
- 1 1/2 tablespoons Dijon mustard
- 1 teaspoon soy sauce
  a pinch cayenne pepper or a dash of Tabasco
- 1/2 cup grated provolone or Parmesan cheese
- 1/2 cup bread crumbs
- 2 pounds walleye fillets
  salt
  pepper

Directions:

In a pan, sauté the onion and green pepper in butter until tender. Add the lemon juice, mustard, soy sauce, and cayenne pepper or Tabasco. Mix in the cheese and bread crumbs.

Line a broiling pan with aluminum foil. Salt and pepper the fillets and place them in the pan. Position the pan 4 inches (10 cm) away from the heat source. Broil the fillets for five minutes.

Turn over the fillets and brush each one with the onion-and-green-pepper mixture. Broil for another six to eight minutes. Serve.

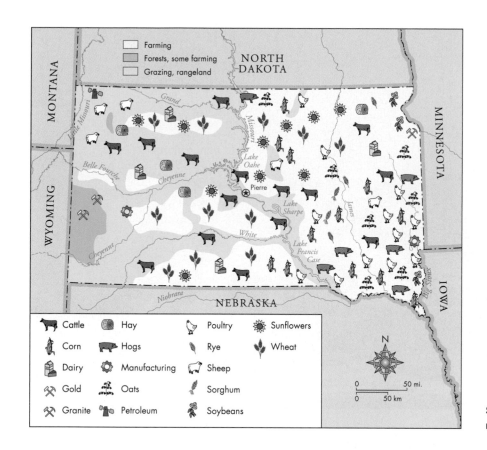

Map legend:

- Farming
- Forests, some farming
- Grazing, rangeland

Map labels: MONTANA, NORTH DAKOTA, MINNESOTA, WYOMING, IOWA, NEBRASKA, Pierre

Rivers and lakes: Little Missouri, Grand, Missouri, Belle Fourche, Cheyenne, Lake Oahe, Lake Sharpe, White, James, Lake Francis Case, Big Sioux, Niobrara

Legend:
- Cattle
- Corn
- Dairy
- Gold
- Granite
- Hay
- Hogs
- Manufacturing
- Oats
- Petroleum
- Poultry
- Rye
- Sheep
- Sorghum
- Soybeans
- Sunflowers
- Wheat

N

0   50 mi.
0   50 km

South Dakota's
natural resources

People at Work

In South Dakota, the service industry employs 83,000 people. This figure includes those who work for the biggest employer in the state, Avera McKennan Hospital, and those who work in their own small businesses, like the many fishing guides in the Black Hills.

About 87,000 people work in marketing and sales. They work at everything from exporting wheat to Japan to selling buffalo burgers at truck-stop restaurants. Tourism provides jobs for 27,500 South Dakotans.

The Avera McKennan Hospital is the state's largest employer.

Job opportunities are limited in rural South Dakota. People there often work in temporary positions. During hunting season, for example, people can earn added income by cleaning pheasants or ducks for visiting hunters. The planting, harvesting, cattle roundup, and tourist seasons provide more opportunities for part-time work.

Other unusual jobs that keep hardworking South Dakotans busy include working as cowhands, fossil hunters, mountain sculptors, veterinarians for bison, casino dealers, gold miners, and jet pilots at Ellsworth Air Force Base. As South Dakota builds its future, it looks to finance and tourism as areas of economic growth.

South Dakota's future
includes farming and
much more.

Computers have changed the way people in South Dakota live and work—and will continue to do so even more dramatically in the future. Many people throughout the country now telecommute; they do their jobs on computers at home. Telecommuters do not have to live near their companies' main offices—they can live wherever they want. As more people find it possible to live and work in the pleasant small cities and towns of South Dakota, the state's economy will continue to grow.

CHAPTER NINE

An Alliance of Friends

A man from a large East Coast city commented how surprised he was when he first moved to South Dakota. "There is so little [of the] free-floating, people-to-people hostility that I was used to finding in crowded cities. People here aren't afraid of other people; they trust other people. Their word is good. It's like turning the clock back twenty years."

That good feeling may be one of the reasons why the state is growing. From 1990 to 1998, the population increased 6.1 percent to a total of 738,171 people. With new businesses moving into the state, people being more able to choose where they want to live, and retirees looking for a good and affordable lifestyle, South Dakota is attracting people from other states and countries.

South Dakota residents are said to be friendly and personable.

Opposite: A South Dakota mom and her sons

Who Are the South Dakotans?

When South Dakotans are asked what makes life good, they tend to answer "family and work." Ninety percent of the farms in the state are family owned. Family members depend on one another and work together. In about 75 percent of families, both parents are in the workforce. Only about 10 percent of the state's families are single-parent families.

More than 90 percent of South Dakotans are white. Many are of German, Irish, Czech, or Scandinavian heritage, descendants of the early sodbusters. About 70,000 Native Americans live in South Dakota, three times as many as lived here before the first fur traders came in the eighteenth century. Only about 3,000 African-American, 3,000 Asian, and 5,000 Hispanic people live in South Dakota.

Population of South Dakota's Major Cities (1990)	
Sioux Falls	100,814
Rapid City	54,523
Aberdeen	24,927
Watertown	17,592
Brookings	16,270
Mitchell	13,798
Pierre	12,906

A Czech festival in Tabor

Throughout the year, South Dakotans honor their heritage in many Native American and European celebrations. Summer is Indian festival and powwow time. Another special day is the second Monday in October. While most of the nation celebrates Columbus Day, South Dakotans celebrate Native American Day.

Christianity is the major religion in South Dakota. Most people follow the Lutheran and Roman Catholic faiths. On the reservations, too, most people are Christians, mainly Roman Catholics. Some Native Americans still practice some of the religious ways of their ancestors, however, and take part in sacred rituals, such as vision quests. For some, these practices are based on a deep spiritual belief; for others, it is an important way to keep close to their cultural heritage.

Celebrating tradition at a powwow

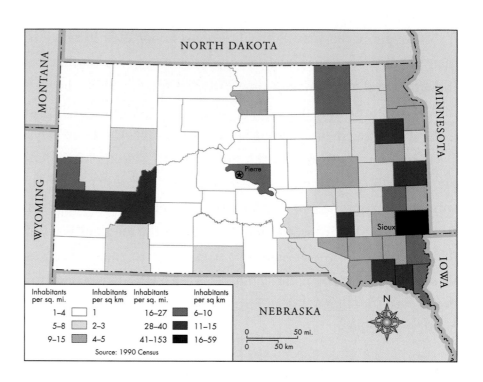

South Dakota's population density

Map Legend

Inhabitants per sq. mi.	Inhabitants per sq km	Inhabitants per sq. mi.	Inhabitants per sq km
1–4	1	16–27	6–10
5–8	2–3	28–40	11–15
9–15	4–5	41–153	16–59

Source: 1990 Census

Living in South Dakota

Today, about half of South Dakota's people live in towns; the other half live in rural areas. More people than ever before are leaving the farms and moving to towns. There is as much land being farmed as ever, but because of new machinery and methods, farming requires fewer workers.

At least one-quarter of the population lives in Sioux Falls, Rapid City, and Aberdeen—the only towns that have 25,000 people or more. West River is less densely populated than East River. The northwest corner of the state is the least densely populated area, having only one person per square mile.

About three-fourths of the state's Native Americans live on reservations. Most of those who live off the reservations need to be

Many people in South Dakota live in rural areas.

closer to their jobs—but they maintain ties to their reservations. There are nine reservations in South Dakota. Only six still have large tracts of land.

Western Living

Although the days of the Wild West are gone, the Western lifestyle lives on. Horseback riding, hayrides, chuck-wagon suppers, rodeos, barbecues, fiddle playing, sing-alongs, square dancing, and pow-wows liven up South Dakota.

Marching bands come from all over the United States and Canada to compete in the Dakota Days Band Festival. State and county fairs draw crowds of people eager to show off and compare their livestock and produce, canned and baked goods. Rodeos often take place at these fairs. Rodeos are contests between cowhands in the traditional skills of bronco and bull riding, steer wrestling, and calf roping.

Casey Tibbs

Casey Tibbs was born in 1929 on a ranch northwest of Fort Pierre. He grew up around horses, and at age fourteen, he began traveling from rodeo to rodeo, "busting" broncos and winning prizes. At nineteen, he became the youngest National Saddle Bronco Busting Champion. Over the next ten years, he won nine national riding championships—a record that is still unmatched. Casey traveled the world promoting the American cowboy and professional rodeos.

His talents weren't limited to horses, however. The rodeo star's success led him to write a national newspaper column. The newspaper column in turn led him to Hollywood, where he wrote, produced, and starred in several movies. He especially enjoyed working as a stunt man in television and movies.

Casey Tibbs died in 1990. The Casey Tibbs South Dakota Rodeo Center is being built in Fort Pierre in his honor. ■

Fishing and hunting have long been popular activities in South Dakota. Many lakes and rivers in the state are stocked with hatchery fish—but it has become difficult to find places to hunt.

In the past, farmers throughout the countryside allowed people to hunt on their fields. Now, farmers have discovered that wealthy sportsmen from all over the United States will pay to hunt on their land. Hunting by visitors has become an important source of income for farmers. Even the state government makes money on big-city hunters. When the herd gets too large in Custer State Park, hunters pay up to $3,000 to hunt bison there. Local people can no longer afford to hunt on their own hunting grounds. Some state land has recently been set aside for local hunters—but not enough to meet the demand.

Excellence in Education

Fishing at Lake Herman

The first public school was built in Bon Homme in 1860, when the state was still part of the Dakota Territory. It didn't last long, however. Three months later, the people tore down the school. They needed the logs to build a fort to protect them against Indian attacks. Those days are gone, though, and education has been a top priority for South Dakotans ever since.

South Dakotans support education with both energy and money. Their dedication shows in their high-school graduation rate of 88.7 percent—America's highest. The state also has one of

An elementary school in Sioux Falls

Learning New Skills

The state of South Dakota supports educational opportunities for all its people. It has recently started a program designed to teach convicts practical skills that will help them find jobs after their release from prison. Prisoners who have learned technical skills have helped prepare the state's schools for the installation and use of computers. With their new carpentry, plumbing, and electrical skills, others are building homes for the elderly and the poor. ■

the highest literacy rates in the nation. To better prepare their students for the future, South Dakota's schools have America's highest computer-to-student ratio with one computer for every 3.8 students.

All students in the state are taught the same required courses to ensure that they all receive the same, good education. Individual school districts and teachers build on this solid foundation according to their students' needs and interests. The school system emphasizes the importance of writing skills by teaching writing as a part of each subject.

In 1998, 132,780 students attended the public elementary and secondary schools. The state spent an average of $4,621 on each student—and that figure has been rising ever since, as have teachers' salaries. In South Dakota's schools, the only things that are falling are class sizes and dropout rates.

The effort and money put into education also shows in high test scores. The national average for eighth graders on the Stanford Standardized Test is 50 percent; in South Dakota, the 1998 average was 67 percent. High-school students have the fifth-highest scores in the nation on their college entrance tests, and two-thirds of the state's high-school graduates attend college. Most choose to attend South Dakota's state universities.

The state has 763 public schools, 140 private schools, 21 accredited colleges and universities, and many technical schools. Jesuit priests run two schools for children on the reservations: the Red Cloud Indian Mission School on the Pine Ridge Reservation—established at the request of the famous Sioux leader Chief Red Cloud—and St. Joseph's Indian School in Chamberlain.

The University of South Dakota's main campus is at Vermillion. It has excellent undergraduate programs in liberal arts, business, and government. It also has the state's only medical school and law school. Graduates of the school include journalists such as *USA Today* founder Allen Neuharth, news anchor Tom Brokaw, and sportscaster Pat O'Brien. Governor William Janklow and all five of the current state supreme court judges are graduates of the law school.

The University of South Dakota has a national reputation.

CHAPTER TEN

Having Fun, South Dakota Style

Fun is never hard to find in South Dakota. With their many lakes, rivers, fields, trails, and mountains, South Dakotans enjoy a wide variety of outdoor activities year-round. Boating, fishing, hunting, swimming, hiking, biking, rock climbing, and cross-country skiing are all part of fun in South Dakota.

Hiking Around the State

Hiking trails—both long and short—cross the state. Two of the best wind through the Black Hills. The Centennial Trail, which is 111 miles (179 km) long, traverses the Black Hills from an area near Bear Butte in the north to Wind Cave in the south. The George S. Mickelson Trail, which is 110 miles (177 km) long, is part of the Rails-to-Trails project. It follows an abandoned railway through tunnels, trestles, and scenic towns.

The Black Hills offer special walking and running activities too. Each fall, during the colorful days of October, participants in the Mount Rushmore Marathon run 26 miles (42 km) through the Black Hills to Rapid City. Other runners have their choice of a less demanding, 2 1/2-mile (4-km) or 5-mile (8-km) run up Iron Mountain Road toward Mount Rushmore.

In June, the Crazy Horse Memorial Volksmarch draws about 12,000 people from around the nation. Volksmarches are organized

Mickelson Trail is 110 miles (177 km) long.

Opposite: Horseback riding on Mickelson Trail

Billy Mills, Track Star

"Live your life as a warrior," Billy Mills's father told him when he was growing up on the Pine Ridge Reservation. "A warrior assumes responsibility for himself and humbles himself," he said. "And a warrior learns the power of giving." Billy was orphaned at age twelve. In his battle to live a warrior's life, he began running—and never stopped.

He won a track scholarship to the University of Kansas, graduated, and joined the U.S. Marines. While serving, he began training for the 10,000-meter race at the 1964 Olympic Games in Tokyo. In one of the great races in Olympic history, Mills, who was at that time an unknown, not only beat the Australian runner who was favored to win—he broke the Olympic record doing it. He was the first and only American to win the 10,000-meter race. The next year, he broke the world record in the same race.

Mills, an Oglala Lakota, continues to live his life as a warrior, as his father asked, by giving to his community. In 1980, he founded the Billy Mills Leadership Institute to lend a helping hand to other Native Americans. He also serves as a national spokesperson for Running Strong, an organization that encourages character, dignity, and pride in American Indian youth. In 1997, he was inducted into the World Sports Humanitarian Hall of Fame. In 1984, Mills's life story was made into a movie called *Running Brave*. ■

6-mile (10-km) walks, which first became popular in Germany. The marchers start at the visitor center and then climb up the mountain statue and out onto Crazy Horse's arm where they have a sweeping view of the plains and the former Sioux battlefields.

Of course, in a state where the great Sioux horsemen rode the prairies, horses are beloved. Whether they're from ranches, farms, reservations, or towns, South Dakotans love galloping across the prairies and trotting the mountain trails. However, most of all they love sunset trail rides followed by barbecues and sing-alongs under the star-filled prairie sky.

Team Sports

Although it's a sparsely populated state, South Dakota has been home to many top athletes and sports people. Among them are George (Sparky) Anderson, one of the most successful managers in baseball; Joe Robbie, former owner of the Miami Dolphins; and Adam Timmerman, who plays for the St. Louis Rams.

South Dakotans love their teams. Although they may follow the pro teams in Denver, Colorado, and Minneapolis, Minnesota, their most enthusiastic support is reserved for their own semipro, college, and high-school teams. The 1999 Road Runners Little League team rode that support all the way into the Little League World Series play-offs. The Stampede hockey team, the Falcons football

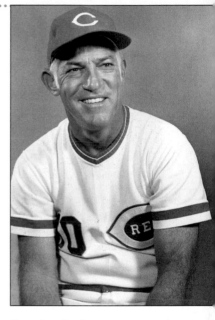

Sparky Anderson, one of baseball's best known managers

Becky Hammon, Basketball Star

Becky Hammon knows all about goals—how to set personal goals and how to score field goals. After graduating from Stevens High School in Rapid City in 1995, she attended Colorado State University. There, she was named Player of the Year three times for the Western Athletic Conference (WAC). She also made the College All-American Team. She holds the all-time season high-scoring record—including both men's and women's scores—in the WAC.

Hammon now plays guard for the Women's National Basketball Association (WNBA) New York Liberty team. The Liberty coach likes Hammon's "positive, team-first attitude." At 5 feet 6 inches (168 cm) and 136 pounds (62 kg), Hammon is small for a professional basketball player. She attributes her success to her philosophy, one that is shared by many of her fellow South Dakotans, "It's important to stay positive and work hard." ■

Black Hills Jewelry

The famous Black Hills gold jewelry was designed by a dream. During the South Dakota gold rush, which began in 1864, Henri Le Beau became hopelessly lost. He thought he was going to die of thirst and starvation. One night, he had a dream about a stream that had grapevines growing on its banks. In the morning, he walked over the hill and saw that very stream.

Le Beau spent the rest of his life designing jewelry that commemorated his dream. Each piece, created with pink, green, and yellow gold, has grapes and grape leaves in its design. ■

team, the Canaries baseball team, and the Skyforce basketball team all draw cheering crowds. Soon, the state will be cheering its new Cobra Arena Football team, which is coming to Sioux Falls.

Writers and Artists

Perhaps it's the wind. Perhaps it's the great sky above the unbroken horizon. Whatever it is, South Dakota has a quality that inspires writers and artists.

Writer L. Frank Baum set his famous Oz stories partially in Kansas, including his book *The Wonderful Wizard of Oz.* However, the tornado in the film version of that book is like the tornadoes Baum experienced when he lived in Aberdeen, South Dakota.

Author and illustrator Paul Goble was born in England, but chooses to make his home in Deadwood, South Dakota. There he writes and illustrates children's books—many with Western themes, such as *The Girl Who Loved Wild Horses*, which won the 1979 Caldecott Medal. Writer and poet Kathleen Norris has also

Oscar Howe

One of South Dakota's most famous artists is Oscar Howe. A Yanktonai Sioux, he was born on the Crow Creek Reservation in 1915. He received his first art lessons from his grandmother, who taught him by drawing in the dirt. Howe later attended Indian boarding schools—an experience that was difficult and lonely for him—but some of the paintings he did there were accepted for national exhibitions.

Howe's early work is realistic—like the early work of most abstract artists—but he is best known for his abstract paintings. Brilliantly colored scenes are swirled together as though the parts had been mixed by the prairie wind.

Although his artwork traveled throughout the world in exhibitions, Howe chose to stay in South Dakota teaching art at the University of South Dakota. He was named artist laureate in 1960 and died in 1983. A photograph of his painting "Sioux Sun Dance" is shown above. ■

Memories of Prairie Life

Laura Ingalls Wilder, who was born in 1867, spent part of her childhood in the Dakota Territory. At age twenty-seven, she and her husband, who was ill, moved to Missouri in search of a healthier climate. But Wilder never forgot her early years on the prairie.

When Wilder was sixty-three years old, her daughter, Rose, finally convinced her to write a book about her childhood. Wilder began writing *Little House on the Prairie,* which led to a series of Little House books. The books were instantly popular, and at age sixty-five, she became a reluctant celebrity.

Wilder's stories are as accurate as any historical documents. By showing the difficulties of frontier life and the closeness of family, they have preserved the truth about the prairie experience and the inner strength of the people of South Dakota. ■

won much acclaim writing about life on the prairie in her book, *Dakota, A Spiritual Geography.*

Two best-selling books about Native American life are *Black Elk Speaks* by John Neihardt and *Bury My Heart at Wounded Knee* by Dee Brown. Neihardt's book presents the thoughts and beliefs of the Oglala holy man Black Elk. Before Brown published her book in 1970, people did not fully understand how much the Plains Indians had suffered during nineteenth century.

Some of our most powerful and haunting historical photographs come from that time period. Photographer Edward S. Curtis traveled around the United States, trying to capture the Native American way of life on film. He photographed many great Native American leaders. Their stories are etched on the faces in his photographs. Today, contemporary artists, such as painter JoAnne Bird, continue to tell the story of the Native Americans in their work.

Actors and Entertainers

Talent is an abundant resource in South Dakota. Many of America's top entertainers and media personalities have come from the state's small population. NBC news anchor Tom Brokaw is one of America's most respected journalists. Mary Hart hosted television's popular *Entertainment Tonight*. Sportscaster Pat O'Brien has hosted the Olympic Games.

Tom Brokaw is a South Dakota native.

Actresses Mamie Van Doren and Cheryl Ladd have appeared on television and in movies.

White Eagle, of the Rosebud Sioux tribe, was a tenor and performer at the Metropolitan Opera House in New York. In 1993, he was inducted into the South Dakota Hall of Fame as artist of the year. Kevin Locke is a popular Sioux hoop dancer and storyteller. Film writer, producer, and director Oscar Micheaux was one of the few African-American homesteaders in South Dakota. In the 1920s, he gave up farming and went to Hollywood where he started making movies that had all-black casts. *The Homesteaders* (1919), the first feature-length film made by an African-American, was based on his experiences in South Dakota. In 1997, a five-day Oscar Micheaux Festival was held in Gregory, South Dakota.

Filmmaker Oscar Micheaux

The Crazy Horse Memorial

Chief Henry Standing Bear approached sculptor Korczak Ziolkowski while he was working on Mount Rushmore and said, "My fellow chiefs and I would like the white man to know the red man has great heroes, too." In 1948, Ziolkowski, with only $174 in funding and working alone, began blasting away at a pink-granite mountainside near Mount Rushmore.

Korczak knew he wouldn't live to finish the ambitious project, so he trained his wife and his ten children to continue his work. Today, the face of the great Sioux leader Chief Crazy Horse stares proudly out across the countryside. When the work is finished, Crazy Horse will be sitting on his horse pointing at the distant hori-

Sculptors of Giants

The two most famous sculptors in American history worked in South Dakota: Gutzon Borglum, the sculptor of Mount Rushmore, and Korczak Ziolkowski (above), the sculptor of the Crazy Horse Memorial. Borglum, who was born in Idaho, was of Danish heritage. He studied art in Paris and gained fame early in life by creating works such as the bust of Lincoln in the Capitol in Washington, D.C., and the torch of the Statue of Liberty in New York.

Ziolkowski, who was born in Boston, was of Polish heritage. He never had any official training in art or engineering. Before becoming involved with the Crazy Horse Memorial, he won several awards, including first prize at the 1939 World's Fair. He worked for a time on Mount Rushmore before beginning Crazy Horse. His other famous sculptures include the memorial bust for Sitting Bull's grave.

Both Gutzon Borglum and Korczak Ziolkowski were great champions of America and believers in large dreams. Each died leaving his work unfinished, but their children continued work on their projects. These men left more than great memorials behind them. They also passed along their skills and values to their children and grandchildren. ■

zon. A model of the finished sculpture stands in front of the mountain so that visitors can see what it will look like. When it's finished, the entire sculpture will measure 563 feet (172 m) high; the face, 87.5 feet (27 m); the outstretched arm, 263 feet (80 m); and the horse's head, 219 feet (67 m).

The Ziolkowski family has refused all government funding. That gesture would surely have pleased the proud chief Crazy

The carving of the Crazy Horse monument continues.

Horse, who never adopted the white man's ways, never wore the white man's clothes, and never allowed his photograph to be taken. Even when he finally surrendered and marched with his people to the reservation, he went proudly, singing war songs. The project is funded by private donations and admission fees to the blasting site, visitor center, and museums.

Those who come to watch the image of Crazy Horse emerge from the rock are watching the carving of history. Someday, Crazy Horse will sit astride his horse pointing to the sacred Black Hills and the plains beyond, to the battlefields where his people lie buried under the sheltering sky.

Centuries from now, people from around the world will visit South Dakota to see Crazy Horse, just as they now travel to Egypt to see the Great Pyramids and the Sphinx. As they try to imagine life in the nineteenth century American West, Crazy Horse will be there to guide them into the past days of the Sioux and the bison. If they listen carefully, they may hear the old songs and ancient stories, and feel the warrior spirit that still rides the wind across the Great Plains of South Dakota.

Timeline

United States History

The first permanent English settlement is established in North America at Jamestown. **1607**

Pilgrims found Plymouth Colony, the second permanent English settlement. **1620**

America declares its independence from Britain. **1776**

The Treaty of Paris officially ends the Revolutionary War in America. **1783**

The U.S. Constitution is written. **1787**

The Louisiana Purchase almost doubles the size of the United States. **1803**

The United States and Britain **1812–15** fight the War of 1812.

The North and South fight **1861–65** each other in the American Civil War.

South Dakota State History

1682 The French explorer René-Robert Cavelier, Sieur de La Salle, claims most of central North America, including South Dakota, for France.

1743 The brothers La Verendrye, the first white men known to visit South Dakota, bury a lead plate on a hilltop near Fort Pierre to prove they had been there and reclaim the land for the king of France.

1803 President Thomas Jefferson purchases South Dakota from France as part of the Louisiana Purchase.

1804 Explorers Meriwether Lewis and William Clark enter South Dakota for the first time.

1817 Joseph La Framboise establishes a permanent trading post in South Dakota at Fort Pierre.

1860 The first public school is built in Bon Homme.

1861 The U.S. Congress establishes the Dakota Territory.

1862 Congress passes the Homestead Act, increasing pioneer settlement in the Dakota Territory.

1874 Lieutenant Colonel George Custer reports the presence of gold in the Black Hills, beginning a second gold rush in Sioux territory.

United States History

The United States is **1917–18**
involved in World War I.

The stock market crashes, **1929**
plunging the United States into
the Great Depression.

The United States **1941–45**
fights in World War II.
The United States becomes a **1945**
charter member of the U.N.

The United States **1951–53**
fights in the Korean War.

The U.S. Congress enacts a series of **1964**
groundbreaking civil rights laws.

The United States **1964–73**
engages in the Vietnam War.

The United States and other **1991**
nations fight the brief
Persian Gulf War against Iraq.

South Dakota State History

1927 Work begins on the carving of the
Shrine of Democracy at Mount
Rushmore.

1934 The Indian Reorganization Act passes,
returning some land and governing
rights to Native Americans on
reservations.

1944 South Dakota becomes the leading
gold producer in the United States.

1960 South Dakotan Oscar Howe is named
artist laureate.

1979 William J. Janklow, four-term governor
of South Dakota, begins serving his
first term.

1989 The town of Deadwood legalizes
modern gambling and becomes a
popular tourist destination.

1992 Native Americans form the Alliance of
Tribal Tourism as part of a movement
to improve conditions on reservations.

1995 Carole Hillard becomes the first
woman in South Dakota to win the
office of lieutenant governor.

Fast Facts

State capitol

Statehood date	November 2, 1889; the 40th state
Origin of state name	From the Sioux word meaning "friend" or "ally"
State capital	Pierre
State nickname	Mount Rushmore State
State motto	"Under God, the people rule"
State bird	Ring-necked pheasant
State flower	American pasqueflower
State grass	Western wheatgrass
State soil	Houdek soil
State animal	Coyote

Rose quartz

State fish	Walleye
State insect	Honeybee
State fossil	*Triceratops*
State mineral	Rose quartz
State gemstone	Fairburn agate
State jewelry	Black Hills gold
State song	"Hail, South Dakota"
State tree	Black Hills spruce
State fair	Huron (late August–September)
Total area; rank	77,121 sq. mi. (199,743 sq km); 17th
Land; rank	75,897 sq. mi. (196,573 sq km); 16th
Water; rank	1,225 sq. mi. (3,173 sq km); 24th
Inland water; rank	1,225 sq. mi. (3,173 sq km); 16th
Geographic center	Hughes, 8 miles (13 km) northeast of Pierre
Latitude and longitude	South Dakota is located approximately between 45° 57′ N and 43° N and 96° 26′ and 104° 03′ W
Highest point	Harney Peak, 7,242 feet (2,208 m)
Lowest point	962 feet (293 m) at Big Stone Lake
Largest city	Sioux Falls
Number of counties	66
Population; rank	699,999 (1990 census); 45th
Density	9 persons per sq. mi. (4 per sq km)
Population distribution	50% urban, 50% rural

A traditional powwow

A cattle roundup

Ethnic distribution
(does not equal 100%)

White	91.60%
Hispanic	0.75%
Asian and Pacific Islanders	0.45%
African-American	0.47%
Native American	7.27%
Other	0.22%

Record high temperature 120°F (49°C) at Gannvalley on July 5,1936

Record low temperature –58°F (–50°C) at McIntosh on February 17, 1936

Average July temperature 74°F (23°C)

Average January temperature 16°F (–9°C)

Average annual precipitation 18 inches (46 cm)

Mount Rushmore National Memorial

Natural Areas and Historic Sites

National Parks

Badlands National Park preserves a dramatic landscape carved by erosion.

Wind Cave National Park is a huge limestone cave in the Black Hills.

National Memorial

Mount Rushmore National Memorial commemorates four U.S. presidents with enormous stone carvings of their faces in a granite cliff.

National Monument

Jewel Cave National Monument protects a multichambered limestone cavern with calcite crystal formations.

National Recreational River

Missouri National Recreation River protects two stretches of the Missouri River and offers a variety of recreational opportunities, including hunting and fishing.

State Parks

The state has a total of nine national lands and six national wildlife refuges. It also manages twelve state parks, eighty-one state recreation areas, three state nature areas, and forty-four lakeside areas. The two most famous national parks in South Dakota are Mount Rushmore National Memorial and Custer State Park.

Becky Hammon

Sports Teams

NCAA Teams (Division 1)

Augustana College Vikings

Northern State University Wolves

South Dakota State University Jackrabbits

University of South Dakota Coyotes

Cultural Institutions

Libraries

The University of South Dakota Library (Vermillion) and the *South Dakota State University Library* (Brookings) are the major academic collections in the state.

The Sioux Falls Public Library is the largest public library in the state, with special collections on art and the history of South Dakota.

The Library of the South Dakota Historical Society holds extensive collections on the history of the state.

Museums

Museum of Geology at the School of Mines and Technology (Rapid City) contains exhibits on the geology of South Dakota.

The University of South Dakota

Sioux Indian Museum (Rapid City) and *W. H. Over Dakota Museum at the University of South Dakota* (Vermillion) have collections related to American Indian heritage and history.

The South Dakota Cultural Heritage Museum (Pierre) contains displays of historical, military, and Indian artifacts to portray the life and culture of South Dakota from the days of the Plains Indians to modern times.

Performing Arts

The Washington Pavilion of Arts and Science, which opened in 1999 in Sioux Falls, presents top entertainers and world-class concerts.

Universities and Colleges

As of the late 1990s, South Dakota had 9 public and 12 private institutions of higher learning.

Annual Events

January–March

Schmeckfest (German food tasting) in Freeman (March–April)

April–June

Czech Days in Tabor (June)

Fort Sisseton Historical Festival in Fort Sisseton State Park (June)

Laura Ingalls Wilder Festival in De Smet (June–July)

July–September

Black Hills Roundup in Belle Fourche (July)

Sitting Bull Stampede in Mobridge (July)

Gold Discovery Days in Custer (July)

Summer Arts Festival in Brookings (July)

Days of '76 Festival in Deadwood (August)

Sturgis Rally and Races (August)

Sioux Empire Fair in Sioux Falls (August)

A Czech festival

Spearfish Motor Rally in Spearfish (August)

State Fair in Huron (August–September)

Corn Palace Festival in Mitchell (late September)

Cheyenne River Sioux Tribe Fair, Rodeo, and Powwow in Eagle Butte (September)

October–December

Buffalo Roundup in Custer State Park (October)

Capitol Christmas in Pierre (November and December)

Famous People

Tom Brokaw

L. Frank Baum (1856–1919)	Author
Tom Brokaw (1940–)	Television anchorman
Crazy Horse (1842–1877)	Oglala Sioux chief
Paul Goble (1933–)	Author and illustrator
Hubert Horatio Humphrey (1911–1978)	U.S. vice-president
Ernest Orlando Lawrence (1901–1958)	Physicist
George Stanley McGovern (1922–)	Politician
Oscar Micheaux (1884–1951)	Film writer, producer, and director
Mervyn Moore (White Eagle) (1951–1995)	Opera singer
Kathleen Norris (1947–)	Author
Sitting Bull (1831–1890)	Teton Dakota Sioux chief

To Find Out More

History

- McDaniel, Melissa. *South Dakota*. New York: Benchmark Books, 1998.

- Sirvaitis, Karen. *South Dakota.* Minneapolis: Lerner Publications, 1995.

- Thompson, Kathleen. *South Dakota*. Austin, Tex.: Raintree/Steck-Vaughn, 1996.

Biography

- Guttmacher, Peter. *Crazy Horse: Sioux War Chief*. Broomall, Penn.: Chelsea House, 1994.

- Iannone, Catherine. *Sitting Bull: Lakota Leader*. Danbury: Conn. Franklin Watts, 1999.

- St. George, Judith. *Sacagawea*. New York: G.P. Putnam's Sons, 1997.

- Wadsworth, Ginger. *Laura Ingalls Wilder: Storyteller of the Prairie*. Minneapolis: Lerner Publications, 1996.

Fiction

- Armstrong, Jennifer. *Black-Eyed Susan*. New York: Random House, 1997.

- Hill, Pamela Smith. *Ghost Horses*. New York: Holiday House, 1996.

- Turner, Ann Warren. *Grasshopper Summer*. Mahwah, N.J.: Troll Associates, 1991.

- Wilder, Laura Ingalls. *Little Town on the Prairie*. New York: HarperCollins Children's Books, 1987.

- Wilder, Laura Ingalls. *Long Winter*. New York: HarperCollins Children's Books, 1987.

Websites

- **State of South Dakota Website**
  http://www.state.sd.us/
  The official website for South Dakota

- **South Dakota Tourism**
  http://www.travelsd.com/
  This official state site offers information on the state's geography and attractions.

- **South Dakota's Popular Internet Sites**
  http://www.sodapop.dsu.edu
  Links to popular sites about South Dakota's sports, arts, government, and more

Addresses

- **Department of Tourism**
  711 E. Wells Avenue
  Pierre, SD 57501-3369
  For information on tourism in South Dakota

- **Governor's Office of Economic Development**
  711 E. Wells Avenue
  Pierre, SD 57501-3369
  For information on South Dakota's economy

- **Office of the Governor**
  500 E. Capitol Avenue
  Pierre, SD 57501-5070
  For information on South Dakota's government

- **South Dakota State Historical Society**
  900 Governor's Drive
  Pierre, SD 57501-2217
  For information on South Dakota's history

Index

Page numbers in *italics* indicate illustrations.

Aberdeen, 71, 108, 110
agriculture, 13, 29, 36–37, *37*, 43–46, *44*, *46*, 49, *49*, 52, 65, *65*, 90, *92*, *93*, 94–95, 99, *105*, 110, *111*
Air and Space Museum, 76
Alliance of Tribal Tourism, 48
American Indian Movement, 48
American pasqueflower (state flower), 60, 91, *91*
Anderson, George "Sparky," 119, *119*
animal life, 19, 58–59, *58*, *59*, 70, 77, 91, *91*
archaeology, 56, *56*, 58
Arikara Indian culture, 15
art, 71, 121, *121*
Audubon, John James, 20, *21*
Avera McKennan Hospital, 103, *104*

Badlands, 10, 13, 52, 65, 99
Badlands National Park, *50*, 57, *57*, 73, 75
Battle of Little Big Horn, *28*, 31
Battle of Wounded Knee, 33, *33*
Baum, L. Frank, 71, 120, 135
Big Foot (Native American chief), 33
Big Sioux River, 66
Big Stone Lake, 53

Billy Mills Leadership Institute, 118
Bird, JoAnne, 122
birds, 59, 91, *91*
bison, 16, 22, *23*, 24–25, 55, 58–59, *59*, 72, 75, 77, 112
Black Elk (Lakota holy man), 54
Black Hills, 10–11, 13, 25–27, 29, 33, 41, 54, *54*, 59–60, *60*, 76, 103, 117
Black Hills cave district, 99
Black Hills gold jewelry, 120, *120*
Black Hills National Forest, 49
Black Hills Passion Play, 79
Bodmer, Karl, 20
Bon Homme, 113
Bonnin, Gertrude Simmons, 89, *89*
borders, 51
Borglum, Gutzon, 41–43, *41*, 56, 125
Borglum, Lincoln, 43, *43*
Brokaw, Tom, 115, 123, *123*, 135, *135*
Brookings, 70, 108
Brown, Dee, 122
buffalo robes, 23
buffalo. *See* bison.
"bumper crops," 94

Canary, Martha "Calamity Jane," 35, *35*

Canyon Lake Dam, 46–47
Capitol Lake, 73
caves, 13, 54
Centennial Trail, 117
Center of the Nation marker, 79
Century of Reconciliation, 48
Challis, William W., 42
Charbonneau, Toussaint, 20
Cheyenne Indian culture, 15
Cheyenne River Indian Reservation, 72
Chouteau, Pierre, Jr., 72
Citibank Corporation, 95
cities map, *69*
Clark, William, 18–19, *19*, 66
Cleveland, Grover, 38
climate, 46–47, 62–63, *63*
Cold War, 76
computer industry, *95*
constitution, 38, 81
Coolidge, Calvin, 42, 56
Corps of Discovery, 19, 67
counties, 87
counties map, *84*
Crazy Horse (Sioux Indian chief), 30–31, 49, 118, 124, 127, 135
Crazy Horse Memorial, 11, 55, 76, 97, 125, *126*
Crazy Horse Memorial Volksmarch, 117–118
Cultural Heritage Center, 73

Curtis, Edward S., 122
Custer (mining town), 34
Custer, George Armstrong, 27, *27*, 30–31
Custer State Park, 55–56, *61*, 62, 75–76, 97, 112

D. C. Booth Historical National Fish Hatchery, 79
Dakota Days Band Festival, 111
Dakota Indian culture, 17, 22
Dakota Territory, 22
dams, 61
Daschle, Tom, 87, *87*, 89
De Smet, 70
Deadwood (mining town), 34, *34*, 78–79, 99
deviled walleye fillets (recipe), 102, *102*
Devil's Gulch, 68
Dinosaur Park, 76

economy, 93–97, 99–100, 103
education, 113–115, *114*
elections, 81–82
Ellsworth Air Force Base, 44, 76, 104
executive branch of government, 81–83
exploration map, *17*

Famous people, 135, *135*. See also people.
fishing, 112, *113*
Flood Control Act, 101
flooding, 47, 101
forests, 60–61
forests map, *58*
Fort Laramie Treaty, 25–26, 37, 49
Fort Pierre, 19, 58
Fort Sisseton, *64*, 71
fossils, 56–57
French colonization, 16–18, *16*
fur trade, 16, 20

Gall (Native American chief), 31, *31*
Gateway computers, 96, *96*
geopolitical map, *11*
George S. Mickelson Trail, *116*, 117, *117*
Ghost Dance, 32, *32*
Glacial Lakes District, 70
Goble, Paul, 120, 135
gold mining, 26, 29
government, 81–85. *See also* local government; national government.
governors, 83
Great Depression, 43–44, *44*, 74, 76
Great Lakes of South Dakota, 45

Hammon, Becky, 119, *119*
Harney, Hank, 34
Harney Peak, 53–54
Hart, Mary, 123
Henrickson, Sue, 56
Hickok, James Butler "Wild Bill," 35, *35*
hiking trails, 117
Hillard, Carole, 89, *89*
historical maps, *21*
Homestake Gold Mine, 34, 99, *100*
Homestead Act, 22–23
house of representatives, 83
housing, 24, *24*, *67*
Howe, Oscar, 69, 121
Hughes, 53
Humphrey, Hubert Horatio, 89, 135
Hustead, Dorothy, 74
Hustead, Ted, 74
hydroelectric power, 45

immigration, 23
Indian Reorganization Act, 44, 47, 87
Ingalls Homestead site, *70*

initiatives, 81
insect life, 36, 43, 91
Interstate 29, 66
Interstate 90, 65–66, 73
interstates map, *69*
Iron Mountain Road, 56, 76
irrigation, 45

James, Jesse, 68
Janklow, William, 83, 88, *88*, 115
Jefferson, Thomas, 18
Jewel Cave, 54, 78
Joseph, Chief of Nez Percé tribe, 30
Journey Museum, 76
judicial branch of government, 81–82, 85, *85*

La Framboise, Joseph, 19
La Salle, René-Robert Cavelier, Sieur de, 16, *16*
La Verendrye, François, 16–17
La Verendrye, Louis-Joseph, 16–17
Ladd, Cheryl, 123
Lake Herman, *113*
Lake Oahe, 101
Lake Sylvan, *61*
Lakota Indian culture, 17, 25
Larson, Arne, 65
Laura Ingalls Wilder Festival, 70
Lawrence, Ernest Orlando, 135
Le Beau, Henri, 120
Lead (mining town), 34
legislative branch of government, 81–85, *84*
Lewis and Clark National Historic Trail, 67
Lewis and Clark Recreational Area, 66
Lewis and Clark Visitors Center, 67
Lewis, Meriwether, 18–19, *19*, 66
literature, 120, 122

Little House on the Prairie (Laura Ingalls Wilder), 13, 70, 122
livestock, 36–37, *37*, 52, 90, *92*, 95, 111
local government, 87–88. *See also* government; national government.
Locke, Kevin, 123
locusts, 36, 43
Louisiana Purchase, 18

Manuel, Fred, 34
Manuel, Moses, 34
manufacturing, 13, 99
maps
    cities, *69*
    counties, *84*
    exploration, *17*
    forests, *58*
    geopolitical, *11*
    historical, *21*
    interstates, *69*
    natural resources, *103*
    parks, *58*
    population density, *110*
    topographical, *53*
marine life, 70, 79, 91, 102, *102*, 112
Maximilian, Alexander Philipp, 20
McCall, Jack, 35
McGovern, George Stanley, 135
Mellette, Arthur C., 38, 71
Memorial Park, 76
Micheaux, Oscar, 123, *123*, 135
Mickelson, George S., 47–48
Mills, Billy, 118, *118*
mining, 33–34, *34*, 44, 90, 99–100, *100*
Mississippi River, 44
Missouri River, 10, 44, *51*, 67, 72
Mitchell, 58, 108
Mitchell Corn Palace, 68–69
Moore, Mervyn, 123, 135
Mother of God Monastery, 71

Mount Rushmore Marathon, 117
Mount Rushmore National Memorial, 11, *12*, *40*, *41*, 42–43, 55, 76, 97, *98*
Museum of Geology, 76
music, 90, 123
Mutual of Omaha Insurance Company, 95

Nakota Indian culture, 17, 22
National Council of American Indians, 89
national government, 89. *See also* government; local government.
Native American Day, 109
Native Americans, *8*, 9–11, 15–16, 19, 21–22, 29–31, 33, *33*, 47–49, *48*, 54–55, 66, 75, *75*, 86, 108–111, *109*, 122
natural resources map, *103*
Needles, 41–42
Needles Highway, 76
Neihardt, John, 122
Neuharth, Allen, 97, *97*, 115
New Deal, 44
no-till farming, 46
Norbeck, Peter, 42, 56, *56*
Norris, Kathleen, 120, *120*, 122, 135
Northern Pacific Railroad, 26–27
Northern State University, 71

Oahe Dam, 101, *101*
O'Brien, Pat, 123
Oglala Indian culture, 17
Ojibwa Indian culture, 16
Omnibus Bill, 38

parks map, *58*
people, *8*, *48*, *75*, *105*, *106*, *108*, *109*, *113*, *114*, *116*. *See also* Famous people.
Philip, Scotty, 59
Pierre, 39, *39*, 72–73, *73*, 86

Pine Ridge Indian Reservation, *8*, 13, 48, 57, 73, 75, 99, 115
plains, 61
Plains Indian culture, 15, 18
plant life, 19, *52*, 54, 59–61, 91, *91*
pollution, 49
population, 82, 107–108, 110
population density map, *110*
powwows, 9, *109*
prairie grass, 59–60, *60*
prairies, 61, *63*
prehistoric life, 15, *15*, 56
prisons, 114
pronghorn antelope, 58, *58*

railways, *51*, 71, 96
Rapid City, 76, 108, 110
recipe (deviled walleye fillets), 102, *102*
Red Cloud (Native American chief), 25, *25*, 29
Red Cloud Indian Mission School, 115
Redlin Art Center, 71
Redlin, Terry, 71
Reifel, Ben, 89
religion, 109, *109*
reptilian life, 58
reservations, 29, 48, 51, 99
rivers, 61
roadways, 56, 65–66, *69*, 76
Roaring Twenties, 41
Robinson, Doane, 41, *42*, 56
rodeos, 111
Roosevelt, Franklin D., 44
rose quartz (state mineral), 91, *91*
Rosebud Indian Reservation, 13, 73, 99
rosebud Indian reservation, 88
Rushmore, Charles E., 42

Sacagawea, *19*, 20
Samuel Ordway Prairie, 72

Santee Sioux Indian culture. *See* Dakota Indian culture.
sego lilies, 60
senate, 83, *84*
service industry, 103
settlers, *14*
Seven Council Fire, 17
Shoshone Indian culture, 20
Shrine of Democracy, 42, 56
Shrine to Music Museum, 65–66, *66*
Sioux Falls, 13, 53, 66–68, *67*, 108, 110
Sioux Falls Air Force Training Base, 44
Sioux Indian culture, 9, 13, 16–17, 19, 22, 25, 124
Sioux Sun Dance (Oscar Howe), 121, *121*
Sitting Bull (Sioux Indian chief), *29*, 30–32, 49, 72, *72*, 135
de Smet, Fr. Pierre-Jean, 26, *26*
soapweed, 60
sodbusters, *24*, 49, 108
South Dakota Cultural Heritage Center, 124
South Dakota State University, 70
space age, 45, *45*
Spanish colonization, 18
Spearfish, 79
Spearfish Canyon, 79
Spencer, 47
Spirit Mound, 66
sports, 112, 117, 119–120, *119*
St. Joseph's Indian School, 115
Standing Bear, Henry (Native American chief), 124

Standing Rock Indian Reservation, 20, 72
state capitol, *80*, *81*, 86, *86*
state flags, 90, *90*
state flower, 60
state nicknames, 54, 63
state seal, 90, *90*
state song, 90
state symbols, 91, *91*
statehood, 37–38
Stavkirke (Chapel in the Hills), 76–77
Storybook Land, 71
Sturgis, 13, 79
supreme court, 85, *85*
Sylvan Lake, 62

taxation, 94, 96
tepees, 18, *18*
telecommuters, 105
Terry, Alfred H., 30
Teton Sioux Indian culture. *See* Lakota Indian culture.
Tibbs, Casey, 112, *112*
topographical map, *53*
tornadoes, 47, 62
tourism, 78–79, 97, 99, 103

University of South Dakota, 65, 88, 115, *115*, 121
USA Today (newspaper), 97, 115

Van Doren, Mamie, 123
Vermillion, 65
volksmarches, 117–118

Waitt, Ted, 96–97, *96*
Wall, 74

Wall Drugstore, 74, *74*
Washington Pavilion of Arts and Science, 13, 66–67
Watertown, 70–71, 108
White Eagle. *See* Moore, Mervyn.
Wilder, Laura Ingalls, 70, 122, *122*
wildlife. *See* animal life; insect life; marine life; plant life; prehistoric life; reptilian life.
Wind Cave, 54, 78
"winter count," 16
Wonderful Wizard of Oz (L. Frank Baum), 120
World War I, 41
World War II, 43–44
Wounded Knee, 41, 48
Wounded Knee Creek, 33
Wounded Knee National Memorial and Massacre Site, 75
Wovoka (Paiute Indian prophet), 32

Yankton, *23*, 66
Yankton Indian culture. *See* Nakota Indian culture.
Yanktonnais Sioux Indian culture. *See* Nakota Indian culture.
Year of Reconciliation, 48
Yellowstone (steamboat), 20

Ziolkowski, Korczak, 124–125, *125*
Zitkala-Sa. *See* Bonnin, Gertrude Simmons.

Meet the Author

When Children's Press asked if I wanted to write the book *America the Beautiful: South Dakota,* I jumped at the opportunity. Although my own experience with the state was limited, South Dakota plays a large part in my family's history. Both sets of my grandparents farmed in East River country, and both my parents were born there. I delighted in walking the streets they might have walked and watching the same horizon they might have watched as they looked for storm clouds gathering to run across the sky.

When writing about a place, more than facts and descriptions must flow from the writer's pen. It's important to capture the spirit of the place. That was easy in South Dakota. South Dakota's spirit shimmers in the air above the prairies and floats among the Black Hills forests. Its energy makes everything seem possible. Perhaps that feeling comes from the great sense of distance and freedom

that surrounds you—in South Dakota, all horizons are far away. Perhaps it comes from the state's rich and colorful history. Perhaps it comes from the busy farms where new crops are growing or from the ancient Native American traditions that teach us to honor the land and every living thing on it.

My travels in South Dakota left me with many great memories: the smell of sprouting corn in springtime fields, the cooling breeze on a hot Sioux Falls night, the crunch of snow in the grasslands outside of Pierre, the excitement of seeing my first pronghorn antelope in the Badlands and bison in Custer State Park.

This is the first book I have written in which I extensively used the Internet for research. The state of South Dakota sponsors many informative websites. With the help of e-mail, I was able to set up interviews in South Dakota and contact people to get detailed answers to questions. It seemed as if no South Dakotan was ever too busy to answer e-mail or phone calls, meet with me, or help in any way possible. On the Internet each morning, I was able to read the *Argus Leger,* the Sioux Falls newspaper, check the latest high-school sports scores, and observe the weather by Web Camera. It was delightfully like being a neighbor of South Dakota—even though I live in Alaska. When not writing and traveling, I teach writing and literature at the University of Alaska.

Photo Credits

Photographs ©:

AP/Wide World Photos: 123 top, 135 (Jim Cooper), 125 (Crazy Horse Archives), 84 (Doug Dreyer), 119 bottom, 133 (Ron Frehm), 44, 56, 97, 112, 118, 119 top, 120 bottom, 123 bottom

Buddy Mays/Travel Stock: 126

Clint Farlinger: 6 top right, 50, 120 top

Corbis-Bettmann: 96 (Layne Kennedy), 43 (UPI), 19, 21, 24, 32, 33, 35 left, 40, 41, 45, 89 top, 122

Dave G. Houser: 73 (Jan Butchofsky-Houser), 6 bottom, 72, 74

Dembinsky Photo Assoc.: 58 (Mark J. Thomas)

Envision: 102 (Steven Needham)

Gene Ahrens: 68, 77

Greg Latza: 2, 7 top, 46, 48, 49, 52, 56 bottom, 59, 60 bottom, 63, 64, 66, 67, 75, 86, 91 center, 92, 93, 95, 101, 104, 105, 106, 107, 108, 111, 113, 114, 116, 117, 132 top, 134 bottom

H. Armstrong Roberts, Inc.: back cover (G. Ahrens), 61 (J. Blank), 57 (E. Cooper), 6 top left, 12 (R. Kord), cover (F. Sieb)

Indian Arts and Crafts Board, U.S. Department of the Interior, Sioux Indian Museum, Rapid City, SD: 121 (transparency courtesy of Mrs. Howe, University of South Dakota/Oscar Howe Retrospective Collection)

Kent and Donna Dannen: 6 top center, 54, 55, 91 top

Liaison Agency, Inc.: 87 (Terry Ashe/Gamma), 81 (Etienne Demalglaive), 8, 109 (Jean-Marc Giboux/Gamma), 131 bottom, 65 (Erik Hildebrandt), 29, 35 right (Hulton-Getty)

North Wind Picture Archives: 60 top (N. Carter), 7 bottom, 14, 15, 22 bottom, 25, 26, 27, 28

South Dakota Governor's Office: 88

South Dakota Lieutenant Governor's Office: 89 bottom

South Dakota Secretary of State: 90 bottom

South Dakota State Historical Society, State Archives: 37, 39, 42, 71

South Dakota Tourism: 70

Stock Montage, Inc.: 31 (The Newberry Library), 16, 18, 23 top, 34

Superstock, Inc.: 51

Supreme Court of South Dakota: 85

Tom Stack & Associates: 9 (John Shaw)

University of South Dakota: 115, 134 top (University Relations)

Visuals Unlimited: 98, 132 bottom (Francis/Donna Caldwell), 80, 130 (Mark E. Gibson), 91 bottom, 131 top (L.S. Stepanowicz), 78 (Charles Sykes), 100 (William J. Weber)

Maps by XNR Productions, Inc.